the ART of
American Game
CALLS

★ **DUCK**
★ **GOOSE**
★ **TURKEY**
★ **& MORE**

IDENTIFICATION & VALUES

Russell E. Lewis

COLLECTOR BOOKS
A Division of Schroeder Publishing Co., Inc.

The current values in this book should be used only as a guide. They are not intended to set prices, which vary from one section of the country to another. Auction prices as well as dealer prices vary greatly and are affected by condition as well as demand. Neither the author nor the publisher assumes responsibility for any losses that might be incurred as a result of consulting this guide.

On the front cover:

Row 1:   Ken Martin Goose Call

Row 2:   Left, Trutone Duck Call
Natural Duck Call
Unknown duck call

Row 3:   Smith T-12 Turkey Call
Korando Cane duck call
Lynch's World Champion Turkey Call
Mallardtone Fox Call
Kolter Yelper

Lower left: Perdew Crow Call

On the back cover:

Row 1:   Herter's Model 99 Squirrel Call
Mallardtone Deer Call

Row 2:   P.S. Olt Perfect Crow Call
Gene Parrish Duck Call
Faulk's Pintail Whistle
Todd A. Goose Flute
Crawford box Turkey Call

Row 3:   Mallardtone TR-78 Duck Call
J. & C. Breland Duck Call
50 calibre Duck Call made by Joe Jaroski

Row 4:   Schultz Curly Maple Duck Call
Makla Duck Call, maple/cocobola
S.W. Yelper

Cover design by Beth Summers
Book design by Allan Ramsey
Photography by Charles R. Lynch

Collector Books
P.O. Box 3009
Paducah, KY 42002-3009
www.collectorbooks.com

Searching For A Publisher?

We are always looking for people knowledgeable within their fields. If you feel that there is a real need for a book on your collectible subject and have a large comprehensive collection, contact Collector Books.

Contents

Dedication and Thank You

This work is dedicated to Joe Jaroski and Harvey Pitt, the first a great carver of game calls and the second the premier collector of duck decoys in America. Harvey also paints duck decoys and Joe and Harvey actually did some decoys together in the past. Without first meeting Harvey I may have missed knowing Joe and his work. Both of these people know the traditional meaning of the word gentleman and have given freely of their time and knowledge and have allowed me to share their information with the collecting world. Without them and the wonderful support of both of their spouses, we would not have this book nor others I have written on duck decoys and game calls.

I also need to thank Janice Jaroski as she was the "computer expert" that assisted me in getting all of my facts straightened out (any errors are mine, not hers) via e-mail. Joe and Janice even drove their calls to our photo studio at Collector Books for photographing. Janice catalogued each call, verified everything with Joe, and then provided the details for the first section. Any errors in that section are likely mine, not theirs.

Finally, my wife Wendy supports me in all I do and without her I could not function, literally. We manage to run a commercial sheep farm, raise draft horses, and sell thousands of items per year online only because of her partnership in these enterprises. But, even more than that, she allows me the freedom to let me do what I enjoy, a true luxury in life.

Contact Author at:

findingo@netonecom.net or lewisr@ferris.edu

Dr. Russell E. Lewis
515 Bishop Hall
Ferris State University
Big Rapids, MI 49307
231-591-3581

Introduction

This is a book about a unique American art form, the game call. Calls are most familiar to duck, goose, and turkey hunters; however, many other types of calls exist and one has been made for nearly every type of sporting hunt as well as for the hunting of most prey animals. A few other books have been written on calls and the books by Harlan are superb. I authored Collecting Antique Bird Decoys and Duck Calls, 3rd Edition, and it has extensive coverage (two chapters) of all types of calls. Yet very little else has been written on this subject and few know the value of a good call. I am not a call maker but I have used calls for duck, squirrel, and turkey hunting. I grew up in an extended family that hunted, trapped, and fished, and used every possible means of gaining their objective at hand, including the use of calls. As a collector I became interested in the beauty of calls and started keeping a few. The next thing I knew I had well over a hundred of them and the calls became a new collection to go with my decoys and fishing lures.

As a former archaeologist and current author on antiques, the next step was to do research on the making and collecting of calls and write a book. My publisher, Billy Schroeder, asked me to do this book with large views of calls to show their intrinsic beauty and tell you a bit about them. The book is not meant as much a reference as a photographic record of about 300 calls shown in detail. I hope this book offers you quality and views you have never seen in a fashion that allows you to better identify your field finds and the calls in your own collection. No one person can know everything about calls and I am the first to admit I am not an expert on them.

However, I have enlisted the assistance of an expert! Joe Jaroski has been making calls longer than I have been alive, since 1945. Joe has made hundreds of calls, and knows or knew most of the major call makers in America, especially along the Illinois River and parts of the Ohio River and Mississippi River hunting areas. He has a collection of hundreds of fine calls from around the country. Joe was kind enough to drive his calls to the Collector Books photo studio in Paducah and allow Charley Lynch to photograph a precious collection for this book. Joe and his wife Janice were also kind enough to take time to identify each as to maker, value, age, and other important attributes the collector appreciates knowing. Joe and Janice did this out of the kindness of their hearts and for this I am deeply indebted. I only ask in return that if you want to know more about Joe's own calls you contact Joe or Janice at:

e-mail: janicejaroski@onecliq.net or phone 618-542-2543 or 618-542-3307

I am the "factory call guy" and Joe is the individual call maker expert for this book. I feel that I know factory calls fairly well as I have made a specialty of collecting and researching items produced for the sporting trades since the early 1930s. Calls really took on new life after the 1930s due to changes in hunting regulations discussed here. You will see factory calls in this work in detail and color that you may not have ever seen before. The same is true for individual call makers. I have included some brief introductory comments but this book is really about the photos and not the text. Each photo has call identification, value information, and a comment or two about the maker when known. The book is broken into three major sections: the Joe Jaroski collection, individual makers in historical context, and factory calls. Sometimes it is difficult to decide how to classify calls as some people made so many they were as prolific as small factories, such as Perdew or Bishop. However, their calls are in the individual call maker section. Then Faulk and Olt were of course at one time "individuals" that became so prolific, they grew to a factory level of production. So they are covered in the factory section (with the exception of any in the Jaroski collection). One thing about writing books of this nature is that people contact me after a book is published and give me new and sometimes unique information. This happened after my last book dealing with calls and I was contacted by a family member of the Faulk family and now have some more history to share. The same was true for the Mallardtone folks.

As a former working anthropologist and folklorist I am all too aware that much of the data about items such as calls is rapidly disappearing as we lose our current oldest generation. Men and women in their sixties, seventies, and eighties are carrying around with them the best information we have on many of the people and calls represented in this book. We need to talk to them now! We need to document as much as possible while we are able. Hopefully this book will be one example of such documentation and more information will become available for future editions or similar works.

Joe Jaroski Collection

This section shows examples of calls made by individuals and a few factory calls as well. As mentioned previously, some of these individuals were nearly mass-producing calls but did not quite cross over that line, such as Charlie Bishop. Some only made a few calls, some made a few dozen or few hundred. Some were painters that added their creativity to a call carved by another. Some were famous and some are unknown in the collecting world. Many, if not most, of the individual calls are not marked in any way, unlike factory calls that normally are marked. However the experienced collector can usually identify a maker by his style, materials used, sound, or some other attribute. The calls shown below are identified when we were fairly certain as to the maker. Unidentified calls are included and so noted. Any identification made by readers will be included in future updates of this volume and my research in general.

The calls are shown without assigning them to any special region or time period. The first 204 entries consist of the Joe Jaroski collection loaned for this book as well as a few factory calls that I left in this section to continue the continuity of his collection. The sections on individual call makers and factory calls include detailed information about selected makers and call companies such as Faulk's, Mallardtone, and Olt. Here is a beginning tour of the call makers' art as represented in the Jaroski collection:

Walnut duck call, carved face details. Made by Charlie Bishop, deceased, lived in Jonesboro, Illinois. $100

Walnut duck call, raised three-panel. Made by Charlie Bishop, deceased, lived in Jonesboro, Illinois. $100

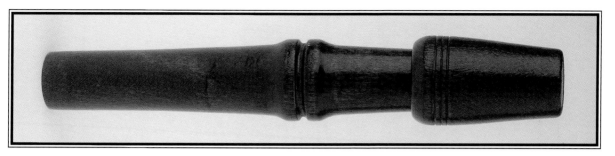

Walnut goose flute. Made by Charlie Bishop, deceased, lived in Jonesboro, Illinois. $75

Walnut goose flute. Made by Charlie Bishop, deceased, lived in Jonesboro, Illinois. $150

Dead Ringer Purple Heart goose flute and reed and stopper details.
Made by Duane Cobert, East Moline, Illinois. $75

Dead Ringer Purple Heart duck call made by Duane Cobert, East Moline, Illinois. $75

Maple Magnum goose call made by Glynn Scobey, Newbern, Tennessee. $50

Magnum goose call and reed details. Made by Glynn Scobey, Newbern, Tennessee. $50

Cocobola goose call, "Pit Boss," made by Paul Englund from Minnesota. $150

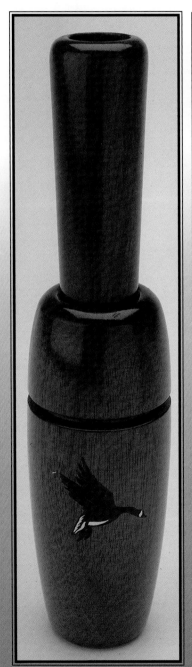

Walnut goose call, hand painted, made by
Glynn Scobey, Newbern, Tennessee. $75

Cocobola duck call made by Paul Englund from Minnesota. $150

Osage duck call made by H. D. Hyatt, deceased. He lived in the Springfield, Illinois, area. $150

Walnut goose call made by Ken Martin in 1989, deceased. He lived in Olive Branch, Illinois, and his calls are fairly well known and in high demand. $125

Walnut duck call and reed details. Made by Ken Martin, deceased. He lived in Olive Branch, Illinois, and his calls are fairly well known and in high demand. $125

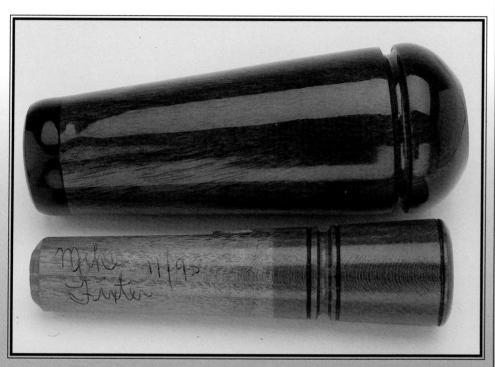

Walnut duck call and reed details. Made by Mike Fixter. $75

Walnut duck call and reed details, hand-painted pair of mallard ducks. Made by J. T. Bucher from Missouri. $80

Walnut duck call with a pair of carved ducks. Made by J. T. Bucher of Missouri. $500

Commemorative call from the 1998 Mid-America Water Expo in Peoria, Illinois. $100

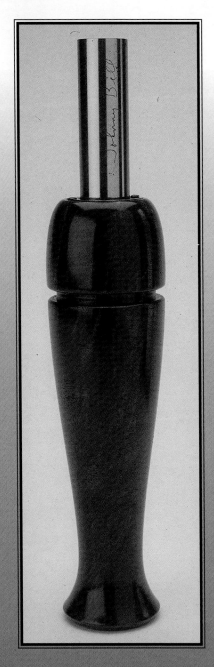

Walnut goose call made by Johnny Bill, deceased. He lived in Anna, Illinois. $150

Walnut duck call made by Johnny Bill, deceased. He lived in Anna, Illinois. $150

Walnut Cajun factory brand duck call. $150

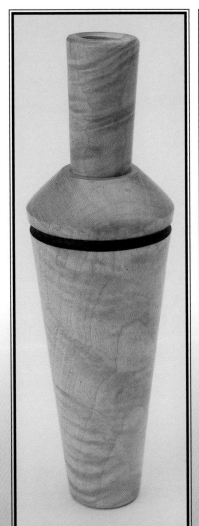

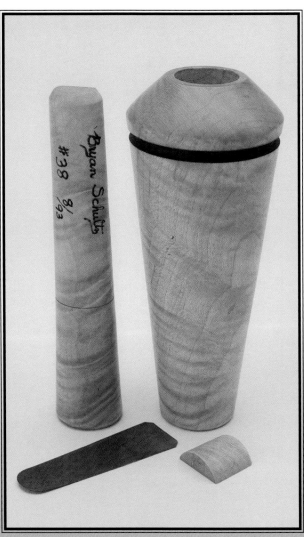

Curly maple duck call made by Bryan Schultz. Details show reed, wedge, and stem details and the Model #38 and Number 8 of 93 calls. $100

Cocobola duck call made by Todd Keeto. $100

Walnut duck call, checkered with duck heads. Made by E. L. Quinn of Tiptonville, Tennessee. $350

Walnut duck call made by Jack Cross, deceased.
He lived in DuQuoin, Illinois. $100

Ebony duck call made by Johnny
Marsh of Tennessee. $200

Persimmon duck call made by Gene
Korando of Jacob, Illinois. $100

Maple goose call made by Rick Perry of Chillicothe, Illinois. $50

Walnut goose call made by Rick Perry of Chillicothe, Illinois. $50

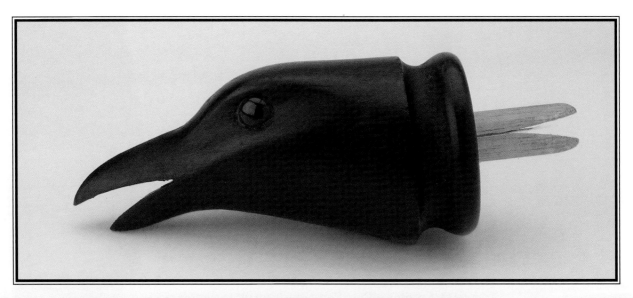

Crow call in shape of crow head made by J. S. Maybe of the Chicago area. $200

Diamond wood duck call made by Buddy Duke of Tennessee. $125

Osage duck call in the shape of a corn cob. Made by Tom Swanson of Iowa. $150

Walnut duck call made by E. L. Quinn of Tiptonville, Tennessee. $100

Walnut duck call with a standing duck. Unknown maker. $100

Maple duck call and details of reed, wedge, and lanyard holder. Made by Harry's Duck Calls, Chicago area. $300

Stainless steel duck call made
by Joe Lares of California. $150

Walnut duck call made by Jim
Blakemore, deceased. $125

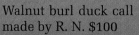

Walnut burl duck call
made by R. N. $100

Cocobola duck call with checkering, heavy duty. Made by Howard Harlan of Memphis, Tennessee. $250. Mr. Harlan is the author of two fine books on calls; see pages 172 and 173 for complete book details.

Walnut duck call, three raised panels and checkering. Made by G. L. Droge of Anna, Illinois. $150

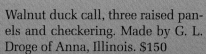

Cherry goose call. Made by Jim Blakemore, Olive Branch, Illinois, deceased. $150

Cocobola goose call made by Tom Weigel of Iowa. $100

Cocobola duck call made by Tom Weigel of Iowa. $100

Myrtle wood duck call made by Gene Parrish of Missouri. $150

Curly maple duck call with a cocobola stopper. Made by Dennis Poeschel. $150

Walnut duck call made by John Lutz, deceased. He lived in DuQuoin, Illinois. $150

Cocobola goose call made by Tim Grounds of Johnston City, Illinois. $150

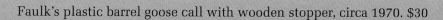

Faulk's plastic barrel goose call with wooden stopper, circa 1970. $30

Walnut duck call with cedar wood stopper. Made by John Lutz, deceased, from DuQuoin, Illinois. $125

Cocobola duck call made by the Killer Call Company. $50

Osage duck call, three-panel with checkering.
Made by Joe Lares of California. $150

Walnut duck call with three duck heads.
Carved by Marve Meyer of Wisconsin. $300

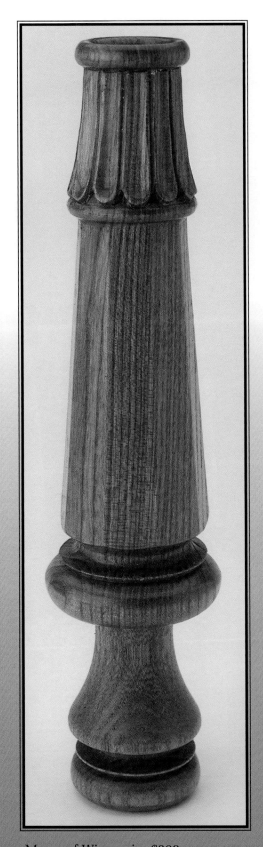

Sassafras duck call made by Marve Meyer of Wisconsin. $200

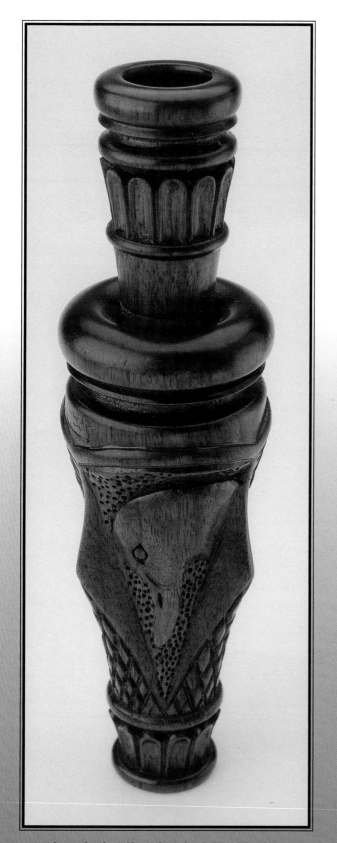 

Walnut duck call with a duck head and extensive checkering. Made by Marve Meyer of Wisconsin. $300

Bubanga duck call with three hand-painted
ducks. Made by Tom Condo of Indiana. $400

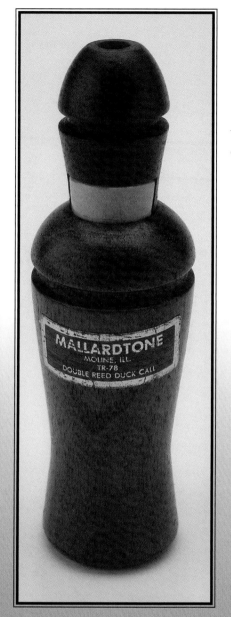

Walnut Model TR-78 double reed duck call. Made by Mallardtone Company. $50

Cocobola duck call. Unknown maker. $50

Osage duck call made by Huggins Hen Duck Calls. $75

Walnut Model DR-66 duck call made by Faulk's. $25+

Maple duck call carved and painted by Kenny Kammerer. $200

Cedar duck call with five carved ducks. Made by Gene Korando of Jacob, Illinois. $250

Diamond wood duck call with whistling wings. Carved by Tray Crawford of the Little Rock, Arkansas, area. $150

Walnut duck call, marked "Sears" on ring. $150

Curly maple duck call with 16-panel checkering, Whiskey River. Made by Bill Bauer of the Seattle area. $200

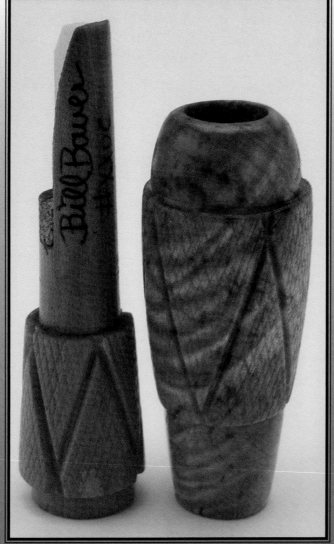

Duck call laminated of various woods, Whiskey River.
Made by Bill Bauer of the Seattle area. $150

Cedar duck call carved by Jerry Reed,
deceased. He lived in Elkville, Illinois. $200

Duck call made from laminated walnut and maple with a cocobola stopper. Made by Faye Holt of Tennessee. $150

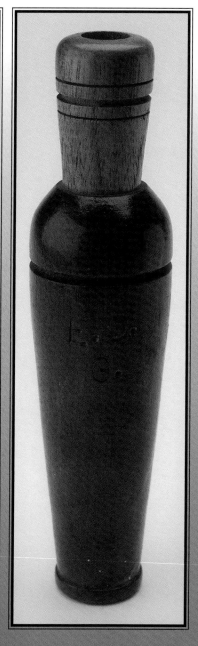

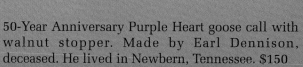

50-Year Anniversary Purple Heart goose call with walnut stopper. Made by Earl Dennison, deceased. He lived in Newbern, Tennessee. $150

Burl walnut duck call made by John
Asbille of Tiptonville, Tennessee. $150

Cocobola duck call made by
D. R. C. Custom Calls. $100

Cocobola duck call made with three-panel checkering. Carved by S. S. $150

Cocobola duck call carved by Jim Hill. This call has six sides. $200

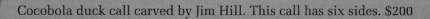

Curly maple duck call and reed and stopper details. Carved by Ray Wright of Alabama. This has four raised and checkered panels. $300

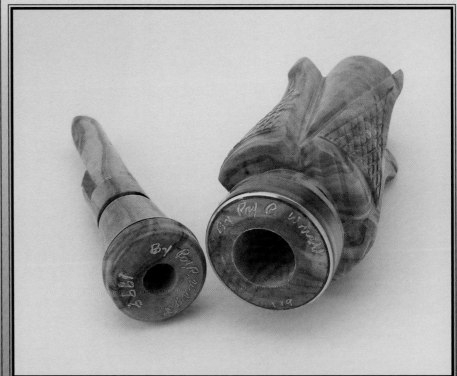

Diamond wood duck call made by Marc Ackerman. $100

Walnut duck call, unknown maker. $50

Cocobola duck call with flying ducks, an oak leaf, and stippling. Carved by D. Almer. $400

Walnut duck call made by Paul McCormick, deceased. He lived in DuQuoin, Illinois. $75

Walnut duck call with a copper band and duck scene. Unknown maker. $100

Cocobola duck call made by L. A. Kotter. $100

Cocobola duck call with double brass band, M. R. G. $150

Cocobola duck call made by Alvin Taylor and called Taylor Made. Mr. Taylor is deceased and lived in Stuttgart, Arkansas. $300

Cocobola duck call with a brass band made by Giden. $150

Cocobola duck call with acrylic stopper.
Made by Webfoot Connection, Texas. $125

Laminated duck call, stopper shaped like 10 gauge shotgun shell. Made by Jack Wilson of Michigan. $400

Laminated duck call with cocobola stopper.
Made by Jack Wilson of Michigan. $400

Cocobola duck call with band. Made by Lommy Loon. $100

Cocobola goose call with a painted goose.
Made by Kenny Meiser of Kentucky. $100

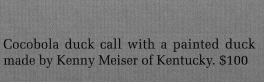

Cocobola duck call with a painted duck
made by Kenny Meiser of Kentucky. $100

Birdseye maple duck call with cocobola stopper. Carved by William D. Makla. $150

Osage duck call with a brass band. Made by Glenn Scott. $100

Walnut duck call made by Art Beauchamp. $100

Walnut duck call, unknown maker. $75

Plastic goose flute made by Rick Perry of Chillicothe, Illinois. $30

Walnut duck call made by Arkansas callmaker. $50

Walnut duck call, unknown maker. $50

Walnut duck call with a brass band. Made by Gene Korando of Jacob, Illinois. $100

Walnut goose call, unknown maker. $75

Ebony duck call with eight raised panels and ivory inlay work. Made by Joel Harris from Southern Tennessee region. $500

Burl walnut duck call with four raised panels, checkered, and with an ebony
stopper. Made by Joel Harris from Southern Tennessee region. $300

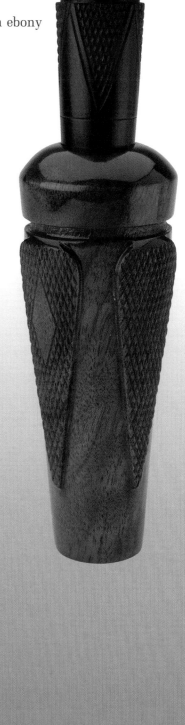

Walnut duck call with six raised panels and checkering. Made by Joel
Harris from Southern Tennessee region. $350

Walnut duck call with carved duck on one side and retrieving dog on the other. Carved by J. & C. Breland. $125

Walnut duck call with two carved ducks and two checkered panel. Carved by Hooker, deceased. $400

Cocobola duck call made by Mike Hill. $100

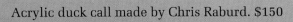

Acrylic duck call made by Chris Raburd. $150

Acrylic goose call made by Chris Raburd. $150

Curly maple duck call with cocobola stopper. Made by J. K. Weatherford of McKenzie, Tennessee. $50

Cocobola duck call with three raised panels and checkering. Made by Ray Wright of Alabama. $200

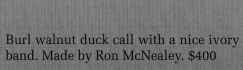

Burl walnut duck call with a nice ivory band. Made by Ron McNealey. $400

Ebony duck call with landing ducks. Carved by Terry Norris. $300

Tulip wood duck call with a painted duck. Unknown maker. $200

Cocobola duck call. Unknown maker. $100

Cocobola duck call. Unknown maker. $100

Walnut duck call made by Big River Game Calls. $100

Acrylic duck call made by Kenny Meiser of Kentucky. $100

Acrylic duck call by Kenny Meiser of Kentucky. $100

Olt's adjustable reed duck call, Illinois. $250

Acrylic duck call. Unknown maker. $100

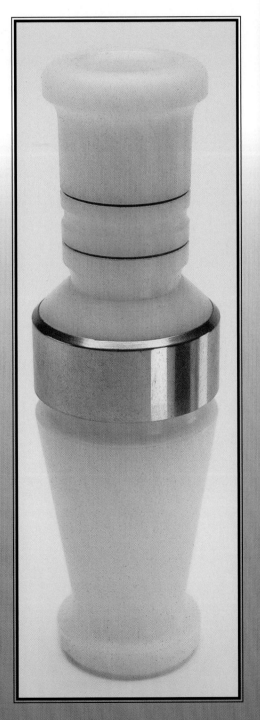

Acrylic goose call. Unknown maker. $100

Acrylic goose call marked "Adrenaline Rush."
Made by Double G Game Calls, Illinois. $150

Acrylic goose call. Unknown maker. $100

Acrylic duck call. Unknown maker. $100

Walnut duck call. Unknown maker. $100

Acrylic duck call made by Timber Mallard. $125

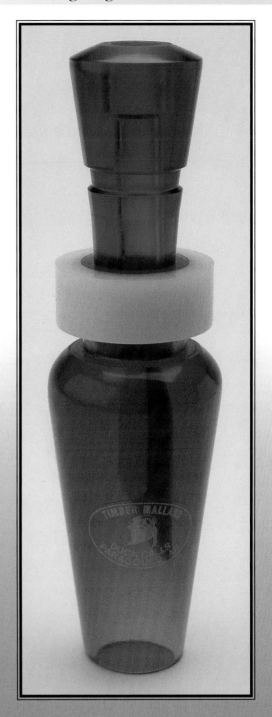

Diamond wood duck call. Unknown maker. $100

Cherry duck call. Unknown maker. $75

Plastic goose call, Victorian Honker. Made by Jack Burns, East Moline, Illinois. $100

Puduck checkered duck call made by B. Woffry. $150

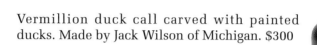

Vermillion duck call carved with painted ducks. Made by Jack Wilson of Michigan. $300

Cedar crow call with carved crow and owl. Made by Jack Wilson of Michigan. $400

Walnut goose call. Unknown maker. $75

Maple duck call with a carved and painted duck. Unknown maker. $300

Nicely carved walnut duck call. Unknown maker. $75

Cocobola duck call in a pinecone design made by J. Dester of Chicago. $400

(Left) Ebony goose call with three checkered panels. Made by Faye Holt of Tennessee. $150

(Right) Ebony duck call with three checkered panels. Made by Faye Holt of Tennessee. $150

Laminated duck call made by Joe Kolter of Iowa. $75

Laminated duck call made by Joe Kolter of Iowa. $75

Acrylic duck call. Unknown maker. $100

Six-pack of Perfectone duck calls and reed details from a Bishop call. Made by Charlie Bishop, deceased. He lived in Jonesboro, Illinois. $300+

Cherry duck call with two carved ducks. Made by Crest Wilson. $250

Acrylic duck call made by Timber Mallard. $100

Screwdriver handle duck call, reed marked #20546. Made by Joe Jaroski of DuQuoin, Illinois. $25

Screwdriver handle duck call made by
Joe Jaroski of DuQuoin, Illinois. $25

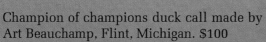

Champion of champions duck call made by
Art Beauchamp, Flint, Michigan. $100

Cocobola miniature goose call carved by
Joe Jaroski of DuQuoin, Illinois. $30

Diamond wood goose call carved by Joe Jaroski of DuQuoin, Illinois. $100

Diamond wood duck call carved by Joe Jaroski of DuQuoin, Illinois. $100

Ebony goose call with six checkered panels. Carved by Joe Jaroski of DuQuoin, Illinois. $300

Ebony duck call with six checkered panels.
Carved by Joe Jaroski of DuQuoin, Illinois. $300

Osage duck call with a painted duck. Carved
by Joe Jaroski of DuQuoin, Illinois. $50

Osage goose call with a painted duck. Carved by Joe Jaroski of DuQuoin, Illinois. $50

(Left) Jack Daniels one-shot goose call. Made by Joe Jaroski of DuQuoin, Illinois. $25
(Right) Jack Daniels one-shot duck call. Made by Joe Jaroski of DuQuoin, Illinois. $25

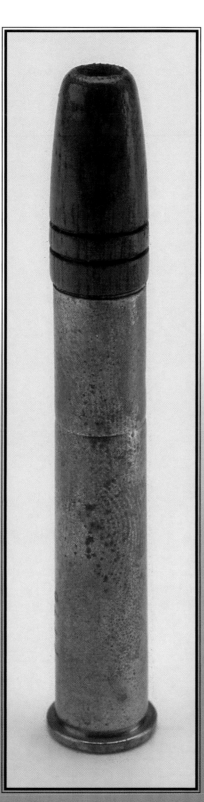

50 calibre duck call made by Joe Jaroski of DuQuoin, Illinois. $50

47-55 bullet duck call made by Joe Jaroski of DuQuoin, Illinois. $30

Acorn duck call with oak leaf design. Made by Joe Jaroski of DuQuoin, Illinois. $35

Corn design duck call made by Joe
Jaroski, DuQuoin, Illinois. $50

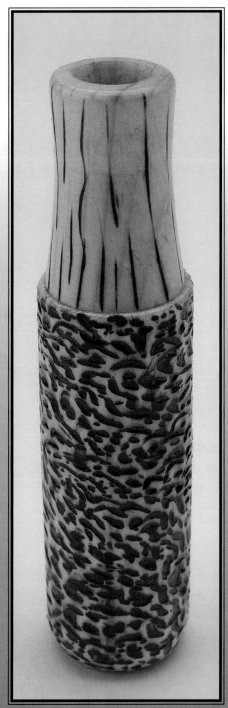

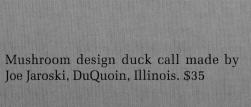

Mushroom design duck call made by
Joe Jaroski, DuQuoin, Illinois. $35

Birdseye burl duck call with cocobola stopper. Carved by Joe Jaroski, DuQuoin, Illinois. $100

Acrylic goose call made by Joe Jaroski of DuQuoin, Illinois. $100

Deer antler goose call made by
Joe Jaroski, DuQuoin, Illinois. $50

Deer antler duck call made by Joe
Jaroski, DuQuoin, Illinois. $50

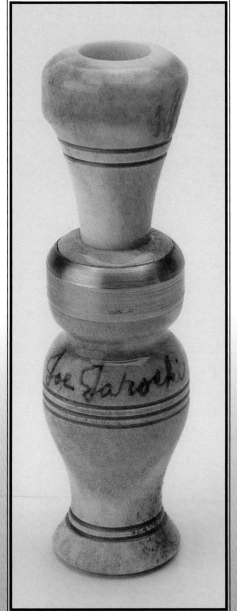

Deer antler miniature duck call made by
Joe Jaroski of DuQuoin, Illinois. $40

Walnut duck call made by Joe
Jaroski of DuQuoin, Illinois. $50

Walnut goose flute and reed details. Made by Joe Jaroski of DuQuoin, Illinois. $50

Walnut Jack Daniels duck call made by Joe Jaroski of DuQuoin, Illinois. $55

Walnut Budweiser beer bottle duck call and stand showing details. Made by Joe Jaroski of DuQuoin, Illinois. $55

Walnut Bud Light beer bottle duck call made
by Joe Jaroski of DuQuoin, Illinois. $55

Walnut Miller Lite beer bottle duck call made
by Joe Jaroski of DuQuoin, Illinois. $55

First duck call ever made by Joe Jaroski back in 1945, made of walnut. Archival item, priceless, not for sale.

Second duck call ever made by Joe Jaroski in 1945, also walnut. Archival item, priceless, not for sale.

Store display duck call made by Joe Jaroski for advertising his calls for sale, 24½" long and made of walnut. $150

A third walnut display duck call, 18" long, made by Joe Jaroski. $150

A second display duck call that is 16¾" long and made of walnut. Also made by Joe Jaroski. $150

Cocobola duck call made by Tiffany Roseberry, deceased, Murphysboro, Illinois. $100

Corn duck call made by Joe Jaroski, DuQuoin, Illinois. $75

Corn goose call and details by Joe Jaroski, DuQuoin, Illinois. $75

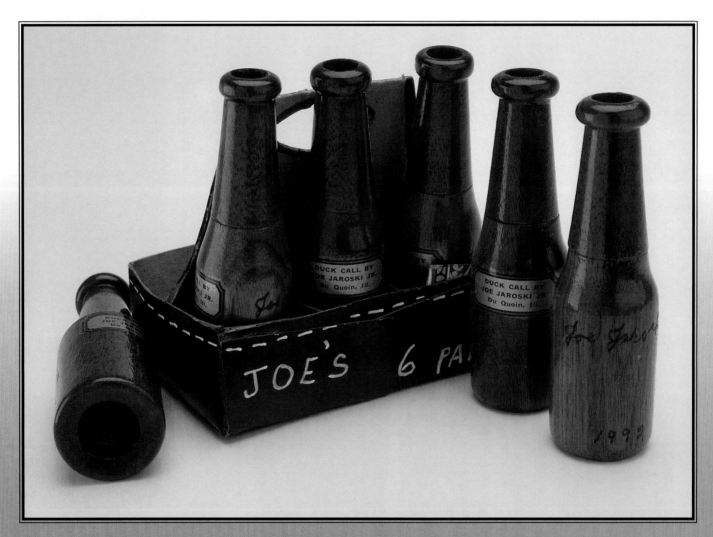

Miniature six-pack of beer bottle calls carved by Joe Jaroski. These are all walnut duck calls. $300+

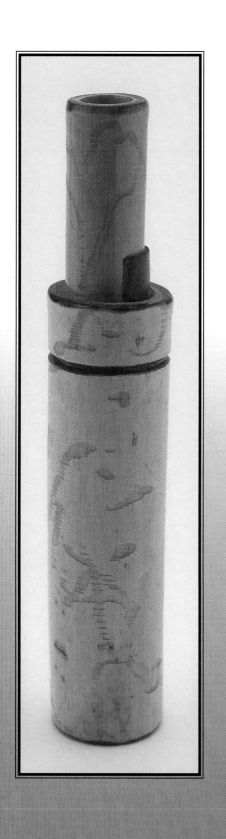

Cane duck calls made by Gene Korando of Jacob, Illinois. $50 each

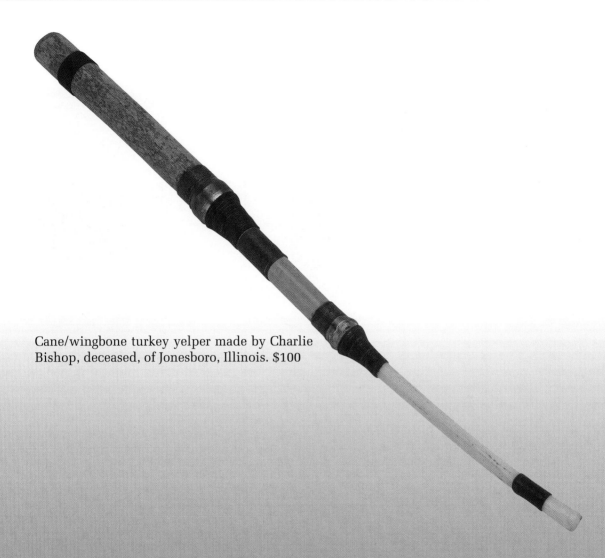

Cane/wingbone turkey yelper made by Charlie Bishop, deceased, of Jonesboro, Illinois. $100

Walnut turkey yelper made by Charlie Bishop, deceased, of Jonesboro, Illinois. $100

50 calibre turkey yelper made by Del Kruzan of McComb, Illinois. $200

Wingbone turkey yelper made by S. W. $200

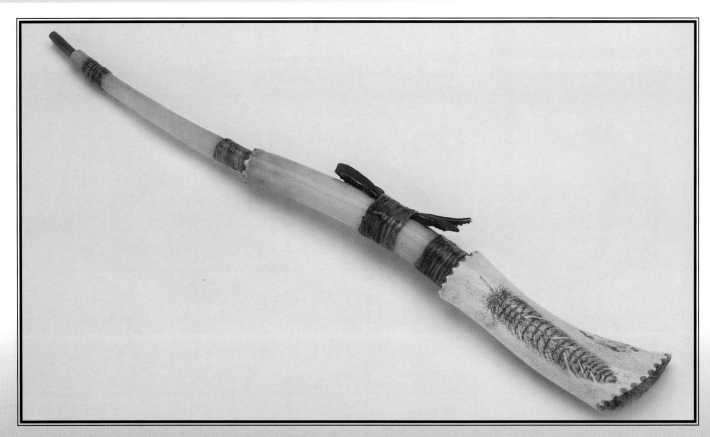

Wingbone turkey yelper. Unknown maker. $100

Osage turkey yelper made by Joe Kolter of Iowa. $75

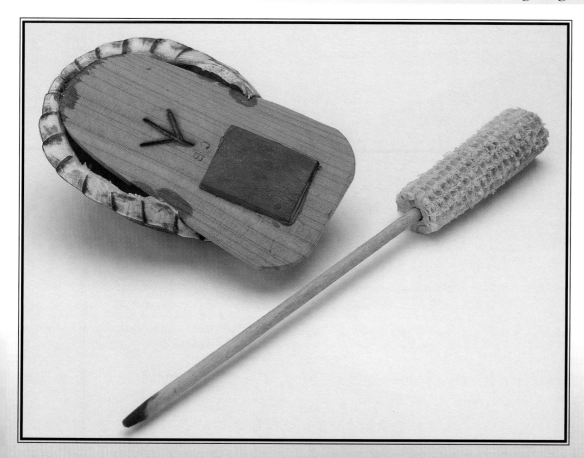

Turtle shell turkey call
made by Charlie Bishop,
deceased, of Jonesboro,
Illinois. $100

Cedar turkey scratch box made by Charlie Bishop, deceased, of Jonesboro, Illinois. $50

Walnut/cedar turkey box type call made by Charlie Bishop, deceased, of Jonesboro, Illinois. $150

Walnut box style turkey call made by Lil' Peeper. $50

Cedar box style turkey call made by Gerald Crawford of Missouri. $75

Walnut box style turkey call made by Jim Groenier. $100

Laminated cedar box style turkey call made
by Gerald Crawford of Missouri. $100

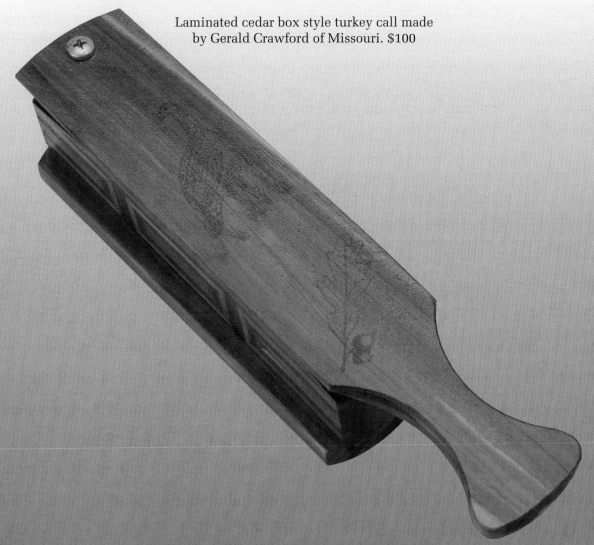

Walnut box turkey call made by Lynch's, World Champion Turkey Caller model. $200

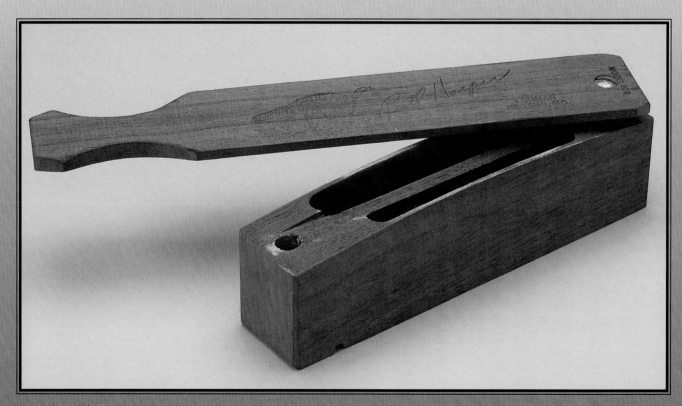

Walnut box turkey call made by Bill Harper. $100

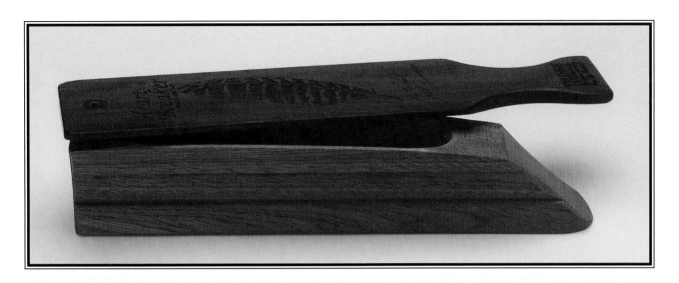

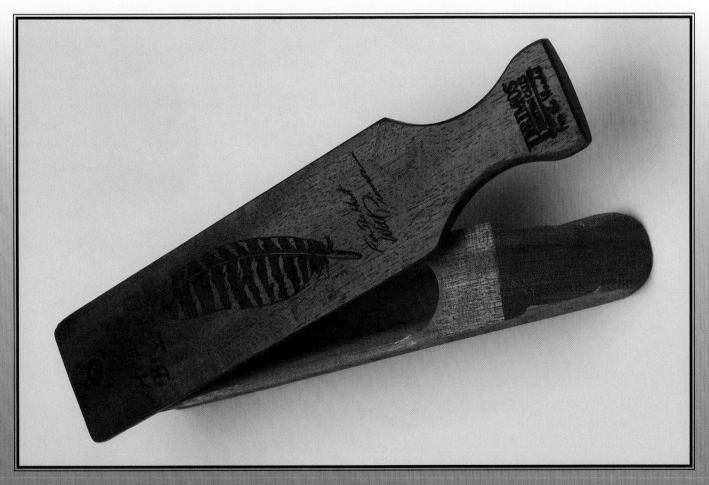

Walnut box turkey call with Purple Heart wood lid, Primos. $100

Goose flute made by Todd A. $100

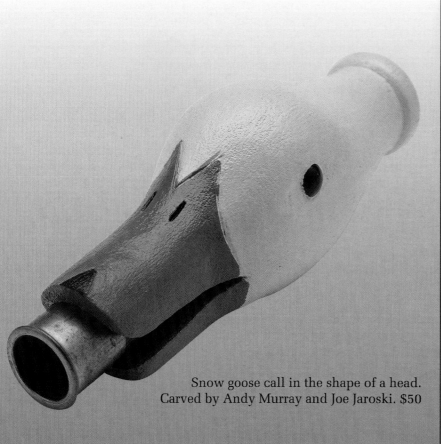

Snow goose call in the shape of a head.
Carved by Andy Murray and Joe Jaroski. $50

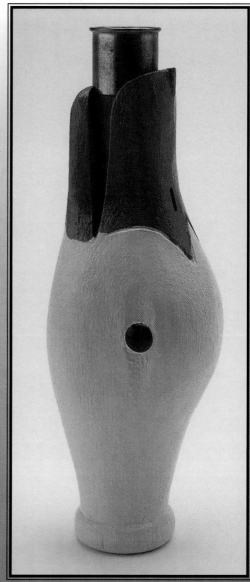

Canada goose call in the shape of a head. Carved by Andy Murray and Joe Jaroski. $50

Duck call in the shape of a head of a mallard drake. Carved by Andy Murray and Joe Jaroski. $50

Duck call in the shape of a head of a mallard hen. Carved by Andy Murray and Joe Jaroski. $50

Duck call in the shape of a head of a blue bill. Carved by Andy Murray and Joe Jaroski. $50

Duck call in the shape of a head of a ring neck. Carved by Andy Murray and Joe Jaroski. $50

Selected Call Makers in Historical Context

1854 – 1870

Others have pointed out an 1854 Currier and Ives lithograph illustrating what is likely the first type of duck call in America, the Tongue Pincher style as first developed and patented by Elam Fisher of Detroit, Michigan, circa 1870, and Charles Schoenheider, circa 1880.[1] A straight reed sandwiched between two rounded or curved radius tone boards bound together without a separate barrel characterizes this type of call. The Tongue Pincher style continued to be made into the 1910s by Fisher and Schoenheider. Others who joined them in the making of these calls were the Bridgeport Gun and Implement, Co. (B.G.I.) in Connecticut, a company named Red Duck Calls, and the N. C. Hansen Company of Zimmerman, Minnesota. They all followed the Elam Fisher design. The Hansen Company was still advertising these calls into the late 1940s.

An example of an Elam Fisher call, from the author's collection. $200+

[1]Harlan and Anderson made the observation that there appears to be a Tongue Pincher style of duck call clipped or otherwise attached to the left breast pocket of a hunter's coat in a Currier and Ives print dated 1854. If you are curious to see the print there is a detail of it reproduced in their book or, if you wish to view the real print in its entirety, you may find one archived or on display in a nearby gallery or museum. The print is entitled *Wild Duck Shooting/A Good Day's Sport*. It is a stone lithograph of a painting by Arthur Fitzwilliam Tail (1819 – 1905). It is not clear if this is a European call or an early American attempt at call making.

Early Illinois River Style
c. 1863 – 1870

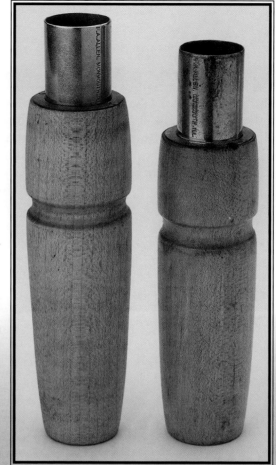

The Early Illinois River Style is characterized by a curved metal reed, a single straight or flat tone board (two-piece stem and insert), a half-round cork wedge block, and a barrel. The first known use of the barrel to create a resonant chamber is attributed to Fred A. Allen of Monmouth, Illinois, and a number of his calls are shown here. His calls are generally stamped on the metal stem, "F. A. ALLEN MONMOUTH, ILL." He was making calls as early as 1863. Others making this style of call were Charles W. Grubbs of Chicago, who claimed he was making them as early as 1868 and advertised them at least as early as 1892, and George Peterson, who was in business in 1873 making decoys and perhaps duck calls. Jasper N. Dodge bought out the Peterson business ten years later, about 1883.

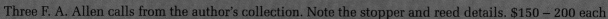

Three F. A. Allen calls from the author's collection. Note the stopper and reed details. $150 – 200 each

Fuller's Goose Call was also made with a similar metal barrel design. The Early Illinois River Style continued to be made into the 1900s even though the variation known as the Later Illinois River Style had been developed and was being utilized in call making, also in the 1900s.

Fuller's Goose Call, from the author's collection. $200

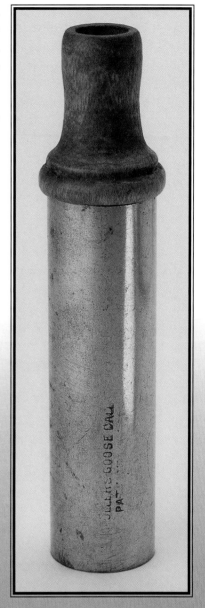

A Perdew Crow Call. Author's collection. $500

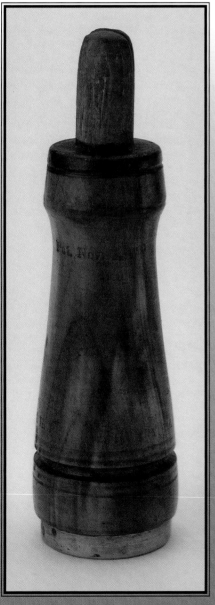

1880 – 1920

In addition to the continuation of the Tongue Pincher Style as mentioned above, the Early Illinois River Style calls continued to be made into this period by Charles H. Ditto of Keithsburg, Illinois (he made other styles also) and James W. Reynolds, Chicago, who became more known for his Double Duck Call patented in 1906. One of the most collectible of all call makers is Charles H. Perdew of Henry, Illinois, who produced calls in the Early Illinois River Style. I was fortunate enough to interview a former neighbor of Mr. Perdew and was allowed to photograph a number of rare items given to him for mowing Mr. Perdew's lawn when he was a boy. However, he could not release them to us for this book as he did not want the calls taken to the studio in Kentucky for the photo shoots due to their value and rarity. These rare items may be seen in both color and black/white in my other book on calls and duck decoys: *Collecting Antique Bird Decoys and Duck Calls, 3rd Edition,* by Carl F. Luckey and Russell E. Lewis, Copyright 2003, Krause Publications.

The later Illinois River Style was developed at the beginning of the twentieth century and it is in this era when the hard rubber call and reed were developed. August L. Kuhlemeier of Burlington, Iowa, was the first to patent this, but may not have necessarily been the inventor. The later Illinois River Style was characterized by a return to the older rounded radius, or curved tone board, and straight reed, frequently both made of hard rubber. They also utilized cork wedge blocks similar to Allen. The calls that represent this style developed to its highest art were those made by Philip Sanford Olt. His company, P. S. Olt, Pekin, Illinois, developed a call they dubbed the D-2 that, with some minor changes, has been successfully made and sold since 1904. The company is still in business today. I have included more on the impact of the P. S. Olt in the next section on factory calls as this is one individual maker that clearly crossed the line into "factory calls." Also, see the rare adjustable reed call in the Jaroski collection.

A D-2 call made by the P.S. Olt Company with the "world logo." This logo was only placed on calls for a short period of time and is desirable. $40+

Arkansas River Style
1920 – 1930

Another style variation is the Arkansas River Style but in many ways it is simply a modification of the Illinois River Style. I do not think we should dwell too much on style types anyway as carvers and makers varied greatly within any one region, often adopting a style or technique they learned from afar simply because they liked it or what it would do to assist their call making ability. At any rate, this style developed circa 1920 and continues today in many areas.

Mark Weedman of Little Rock, Arkansas, started making beautiful wooden calls in the 1930s. His early calls are the most desirable to collectors, but some of the later acrylic models are collectible also. He started making the latter in the 1950s and as far as is known, no longer fashioned calls from wood. There are red, white, blue, orange, silver, yellow, and amber colored laminations making up some of his calls. It and his other acrylic calls are identified by the words "WEEDY'S PIN OAK" found stamped around the top where the stem is inserted.

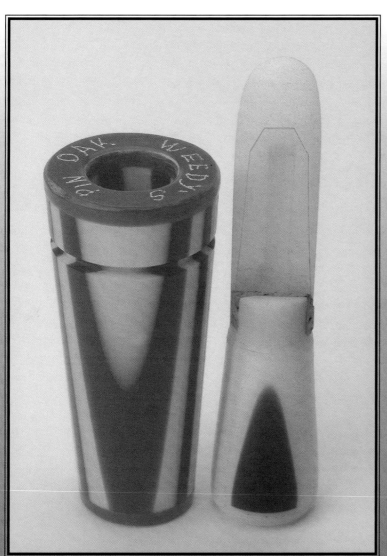

Weedy's Pin Oak call and stamping details, candy stripe acrylic duck call. Author's collection. $100

Louisiana Style
1930 – 1935

The Louisiana Style or Cajun Style duck calls were in commercial production as early as the 1930s for certain. The earliest names associated with the Louisiana Style calls are Faulk and Airhart. Clarence "Patin" Faulk of Lake Charles is known to have made calls much earlier than the 1935 date generally accepted as when he began making calls to be sold in commercial quantities. Although he produced thousands of calls, it was not until 1950, when his son Dudley Faulk went into business, that we recognized the company as it exists doing business today, Faulk's Calls. Another famous name in the Louisiana Style of call making is Allen J. Airhart. He started the Cajun Call Company in Lake Charles in 1944. Although many calls are made of wood and other materials today, most classic Louisiana Style calls were made of cane. They are generally of the two-piece design much like the F. A. Allen calls described and illustrated on previous pages. Faulk's calls are detailed in the next section and a Cajun call was shown in the Jaroski collection section.

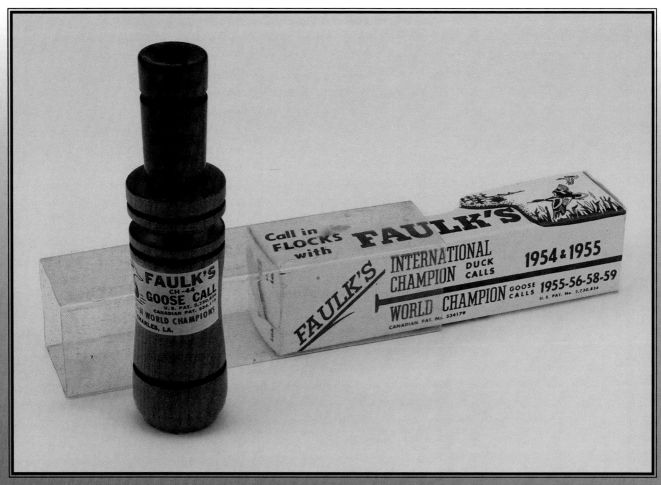

A Faulk's Model CH-44 goose call and box, circa 1961.
Author's collection (box is 1959, call is 1961). $50+

The Golden Age
1935 – 1950

The early historical eras documented in the previous pages contributed to the growth and development of American call making when everyone was experimenting and perfecting what they thought were the best in effective game calls. However there really was not an impetus for large scale manufacturing until 1935. Heretofore using bait and/or live decoys was common, especially in the Mississippi Flyway. Why produce calls in any quantities when you have the benefit of having a few live English calling ducks or Suzys as they were affectionately known? One could actually have the double benefit of live ducks as decoys making live, authentic calls when desired and a few family pets at the same time.

In 1935 two significant things happened that would have a profound and lasting effect on the way wildfowl hunters pursued their prey. First, Ducks Unlimited was formed in the interest of proper wildlife management and conservation. Second, the federal government made baiting fields and the use of live decoys illegal. The previous year had seen the birth of the Federal Waterfowl Stamps and the publication of Joel Barber's classic work on decoys. All of these events had an impact on the current hobby of collecting calls and decoys.

Now, there was suddenly a very good reason for obtaining and learning to use game calls. Thus was born the "Golden Age" of duck call making. Many of the older call making operations expanded to accommodate this sudden increase in demand. They began producing thousands of calls even as new companies were born, also producing calls in the thousands to meet this demand. Many individuals entered the call making business during this era, including the P. S. Olt Company. Also, decoy makers got into the business. The big sporting goods firms such as Von Lengerke and Antoine (VL&A) of Chicago, Sears Roebuck, H. D. Folsom Arms Company, and the like, began commissioning call makers to manufacture calls for sale through their stores and catalogs, some even with their own logos on them. This was also the time when duck calling competition became a sport of its own.

A Model A-5 Perfect Goose Call by P. S. Olt Co., a standard for some time. $75

1950 – 1970s

By about 1950 the wildfowl population had dwindled again. Good efforts were being made at conservation, but they were slow in getting started and gaining support. At this point in time, general interest in hunting waterfowl was on the wane and the number of hunters was declining. There were still many commercial call-making companies doing business at the time. The decline of waterfowl population and hunter interest and the ready availability of inexpensive, manufactured duck calls combined, put quite a damper on the business of hand production of fine duck calls. This depressed situation remained at a status quo until renewed by growing interest in Americana beginning in the 1970s. This ushered in a new interest in "hand-crafted" items, including quality duck and goose, turkey, crow, deer, and other game calls.

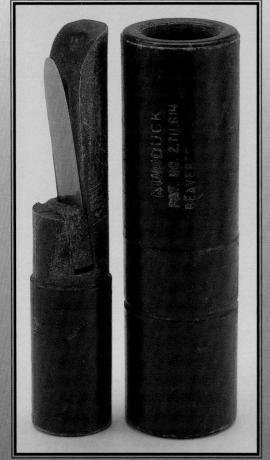

A KumDuck call and details from Beaverton, Oregon, made circa 1955 demonstrates the mass marketed calls being made during this period, including calls made of plastic. $50 (fairly rare)

1970s – Present

The 1970s saw a renewed interest in all things related to American craftsmen, especially those things that were uniquely American. With this came the now famous explosion of interest in old hand-made hunting decoys and all sorts of other Americana. Good game conservation and management had begun to pay off with rapidly increasing waterfowl populations. Along with these conservation efforts, heavily supported by hunters and other outdoor sportsmen, came a new appreciation for what was almost lost — a new appreciation for the sheer pleasure of the hunt, a heightened awareness, if you will, of the experience of the hunt, being outdoors, enjoying it with a friend or introducing a child to the magic. What a great pleasure and satisfaction it is to introduce a non-outdoorsman friend or a child to this world, knowing that you helped bring it back and you and they will continue to practice good game management to assure it will not be lost. Thus, the renaissance of the fine calls. It can only get better.

Greg Keats duck call showing reed, stem and stopper details. A beautiful example of the type of calls being made now by those practicing the callmakers' art. $150+

Joe Jaroski corn cob goose call. $75

Joe Jaroski corn cob duck call. $75

Joe Jaroski corn cob predator call. $50 – 75

Joe Jaroski fancy checkered duck call with a duck and lab hand-painted by Bill Cowey from Centralia, Illinois. Joe also has had some painting done by Ken Presswood of DuQuoin, Illinois. $200+

Additional Calls and Companies

Call collectors need to be aware of modern calls and mass marketed calls while searching for items to collect. Although anyone will appreciate a Perdew, an Allen, or a beautiful old Fuller's, most collectors will find few of these early examples to collect compared to the many factory calls. Many factory calls are nearly as beautiful and some such as the TRUTONE duck call shown on page 167 has few rivals. I hope all are able to fill in their collections with a few fine calls and an early Elam Fisher, but the beauty of early Faulk's, Mallardtone, Olt, Lohman, and other factory calls should not be scoffed at simply because they were "factory" calls. That would be similar to a decoy collector foregoing a Mason because it is a factory bird!

Mass produced calls from the forties and fifties are still readily available and can be purchased online, in antique stores, at flea markets, and even in some sporting goods stores if one is diligent in searching. Many of the calls will still be found in their original one- or two-piece cardboard packaging and with package inserts telling how to use the call or little pocket catalogs. These make great additions to a collection and further one's knowledge on a company's products. Even concentrating on just a few of the larger or better known companies can take quite an effort to acquire all calls known to exist. Even some of the calls of more recent 1970s companies are getting harder and harder to find.

There were likely dozens, if not hundreds, of small mom and pop call companies in the later forties and early fifties that have yet to be documented. My fishing lure research makes it clear that nearly every small community had a small company operating out of a kitchen or a garage. Though these small companies were cheap to start, most did not last due to the inability to market the products widely enough. My review of literature for advertising indicates a few small companies that advertised but most of these little companies lived on local distribution and sales, direct marketing to sports shops, and word of mouth. Again, I request my readers to contact me with any pertinent details on companies not represented in this book that existed at any time from 1935 until 1970. I may include them in future volumes.

DUC-EM

The *Shooter's Bible* for 1947 lists two of these calls for sale, the Pull-Em Crow Call and the DUC-EM Duck Call. Both calls use the phrase "Tone Tested" in their names as well. The 1966 *Shooter's Bible* no longer lists the calls but some sporting magazines still advertised them in the 1960s. The company capitalized in their advertisements for a problem with the Lohman calls concerning the difficulty of putting the reeds back into place. Lohman calls are very nice but very hard to reassemble for a beginner. DUC-EM also advertised duck decoys. They are nice calls and fairly scarce for company calls. They produce a quality sound. Either of the duck or crow call would bring about $75, more with box.

Pull-Em crow call, DUC-EM brand. $75

FAULK'S

Already discussed briefly in the previous section, the Faulk's company began commercial call production in about 1935 in Lake Charles, Louisiana. I have shown here a number of calls made by the company in the forties, fifties, and sixties. Any of these would make nice additions to a call collection, especially the ones still in their original packaging with package inserts. As a general rule, the presence of original packaging tends to at least double the value of an item such as a game or duck call.

One dating technique on Faulk's calls is the company's use of advertising on the call labels, the boxes, and the paper inserts. Faulk's calls won a number of competitions and the company listed the years in which it won on the call labels, boxes, and inserts. However, an interesting thing is that the years often did not match, showing that Faulk's would use calls on hand and boxes on hand and would place updated inserts into the box. One call clearly shows the box as a 1959, the call as a 1961, and a paper insert dated 1963. Thus, the call is really from 1963, likely made in 1961 as that is the date on the call, and placed in a box on hand from 1959. So when you get a Faulk's, look at all the dates to determine the likely date of your item. This does not surprise me, for Heddon did the same thing with fishing lures. Heddon would often use surplus boxes from an earlier year to house its new lures. It would only make marketing sense to use up one's stock on hand to save money.

Another possible dating technique is the box design and/or color. Three boxes from the fifties and sixties evolved with the earliest one being red, then orange, then yellow. The design on the box stayed the same but the colors changed. Also, all of the ones from this period are the plastic slide-top boxes; earlier boxes would have had plastic lids over cardboard or would have been two-piece cardboard boxes. Later boxes may have a cellophane insert as also used on some later Olt boxes. As collector attention is placed more and more on these factory calls, we will learn smaller distinctions in box types to help us date the items and I will include this information if there are later editions.

Below, I have included some catalog data from the 1970s and early 1980s to illustrate model numbers and some pricing information on Faulk's calls. This will give the collector a benchmark of available calls from Faulk's and will also assist in determining general values for the calls. As with most collectibles, the more expensive the item was when released to the marketplace, the more valuable it usually is today to collectors. Thus, the limited edition releases have really gone up in value far more than the calls made in mass quantities. However, all of the calls from the 1950s – 1970s have increased in value and some are very hard to find, especially boxed.

The 1970 Parker Distributors (New Rochelle, New York) wholesale hunting and fishing catalog offered the following Faulk's calls for sale:
1. WA-33 Deluxe Duck Call with walnut barrel
2. CH-44 Deluxe Goose Call with cherry/walnut barrel
3. C-50 Crow Call, walnut barrel, cherry tip
4. P-60 Predator Call, walnut barrel, metal reed
5. Pat. Pending P-60A Adjustable Predator Call
6. H-10 Hawk Call, walnut barrel, cherry tip
7. EK-8 Elk Call, plastic with cork insert
8. CA-11 Duck Call, bamboo (cane)
9. WA-11 Duck Call, walnut
10. CA-22 Duck Call, bamboo with metal ring
11. WA-22 Duck Call, walnut with metal ring
12. Q-20 Bob White Quail Call, walnut with cork insert
13. S-80 Squirrel Call, rubber bulb with metal device
14. D-50 Deer Call, walnut barrel
15. SG-49 Speckled Belly Goose Call, walnut, metal reed
16. WD-30 Wood Duck Call, walnut with rubber reed, advertised as "NEW" for 1970
17. SC-77 Supreme Duck Call, extra large, walnut
18. SCJ-66 Supreme Duck Call, smaller, walnut

19. C-100 Duck Call, myrtlewood and walnut
20. WA-33-A Adjustable Duck Call, walnut with adjustable ring
21. RW-14 Professional Duck Call, rosewood, large
22. PL-22 Popular Goose Call, plastic/wood
23. PH-95 Pheasant Call, walnut, metal reed
24. H-100 Honker Call, walnut
25. Q-19 Quail Call, box type for Western Quail
26. D-8 Dove Call, plastic construction
27. T-40 Turkey Call, a box/striker type call, advertised as "NEW" for 1970
28. Duck-Goose calling record

The 1981 Point Wholesale catalog still offered the following Faulk's products:
1. Faulk's DL (double lanyard to hold two calls)
2. Faulk's Crow Call, Model 50
3. Faulk's Regular Duck Call, Model WA 11 (walnut)
4. Faulk's Regular Duck Call, Model CA 11 (bamboo)
5. Faulk's Special Duck Call, Model WA 22 (metal band)
6. Faulk's Deluxe Duck Call, Model WA 33 (heavy duty)
7. Faulk's Adjustable Duck Call, Model WA 33A
8. Faulk's Duck Call, Model C 100 (fancy zebra wood)
9. Faulk's Pintail Whistle, Model PW 70
10. Faulk's Popular Goose Call, Model PL 22 (clear)
11. Faulk's Deluxe Goose Call, Model CH 44 (cherry)
12. Faulk's Predator Call, Model P 60
13. Faulk's Adjustable Predator Call, Model P 60A
14. Faulk's Model S 80 Squirrel Call (rubber bulb)

The 1982 catalog from Buckeye Sports Supply, Canton, Ohio, another big wholesaler of sporting goods, in addition to the above, offered the following calls:
15. Faulk's Professional Duck Call, Model RW 14 (large, fancy wood)
16. Faulk's Wood Duck Call, Model WD 30
17. Faulk's Honker Call, Model H 100
18. Faulk's Elk Call, Model EK 8 (rigid plastic/cork insert)
19. Faulk's Bob White Quail Call, Model Q 20
20. Faulk's Deer Call, Model D 50
21. Faulk's Box/Striker Turkey Call, Model T 40
22. Faulk's Presentation Gift Set, Model GS 12, contained one each of the lesser models of duck, goose, and crow calls in a gift box
23. General reeds and goose reeds

Thus, in 1982, Faulk's still offered over 23 products for sale in two major wholesalers' catalogs. Most of the calls were wood made from walnut and/or cherry. The clear goose call (PL 22) is plastic and wood. The elk call is also plastic. Faulk's used a beautiful cherry wood and the calls are attractive. They are also easy to use and well tuned.

Again, the more unusual calls to find would be the gift set, the turkey call (just beginning to get real popular in the northern states in the early eighties), the expensive professional duck call (wholesale was $12.45, retailed at $22.95), and the calls for the more unusual species. Most of the above calls were in the Faulk's line for a number of years to allow the collector to amass examples from different time periods. A most unusual Faulk's item was the Big Duck Call, Model FGD (Faulk's Giant Duck). In 1970, Cabela's offered this item for $15.95. It was a giant working call measuring 11¾" overall, but actually properly tuned to work. It was meant as a gift for the sportsman who had everything, a nice item for the blind or bar.

A second Faulk's WA-33A adjustable duck call. Author's collection. $30

Faulk's WA-33A adjustable duck call, mint condition. Author's collection. $40

Faulk's Model WA-11 (walnut) duck call from 1959 in red pre-zip code slide-top box. Author's collection. $50+

Faulk's Model PW-70 pintail whistle/call in orange pre-zip code slide-top box. Author's collection. $50+

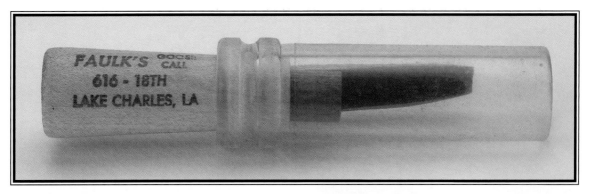

Faulk's Clear Goose Call, circa 1970, shown in 1970 catalogs. Author's collection. $30

Reed, stopper and stem details from a well-used Faulk's. $20

A Faulk's duck call.
Author's collection. $30 each

HERTER'S INC.

Herter's, Inc. of Wasceca, Minnesota, made nearly every call imaginable for prey, sporting birds, deer, elk, ducks, and geese. Most of the calls follow the Glodo style and are so called by Herter's. The Herter's specialty catalogs for duck and goose hunting really detail the calls nicely, but even the general Herter's catalogs list all calls available from the company: duck, goose, any flying game bird, crow, deer, elk, and predator, to name just a few. Not all calls were available for the entire or so 40-year timespan, so one needs to study catalogs to precisely date calls. But this is affordable with Herter's catalogs being available for only a few dollars each. Cabela's recently purchased Herter's so we will need to see what future collectibles will ultimately be produced under the new Herter's/Cabela's partnership.

The previous owner of Herter's still marketed the famous Glodo duck call in an old Herter's two piece cardboard box, so make sure you can tell the old ones from the newer ones, the package being the best guarantee. The oldest Herter's calls had brass rings and bring hundreds, if not thousands, of dollars each. However, for the most part, the new collector is more apt to find nice old Herter's calls from the forties or fifties than one of the very early calls.

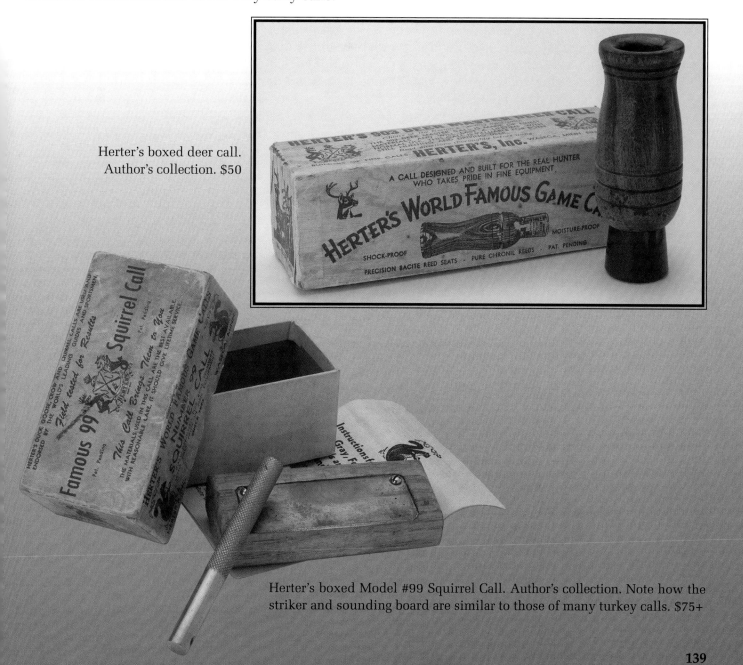

Herter's boxed deer call. Author's collection. $50

Herter's boxed Model #99 Squirrel Call. Author's collection. Note how the striker and sounding board are similar to those of many turkey calls. $75+

JOE JAROSKI, JR.

Joe's Collection is shown earlier, but here is a bit more about Joe and his calls. Joe Jaroski, Jr., was born on February 28, 1925, and is still making calls today in DuQuoin, Illinois. Joe is a man of few words but a fine call maker. This is a story his wife, Janice, shared with me about being a man of few words. "Got to tell you a little story. Joe's grandson interviewed him on a tape about his tour in World War II. There were several questions and the entire tape was only six minutes. I told Joe I could have talked that long on the first question and I was not even there. He laughed and told me I could have talked that long without taking a breath." But actually, the day I spent a few hours with Joe he was very talkative and helped me a lot with my call research. He shared data about calls and call making freely and has 60 years of experience to share.

Joe made his first call in 1945 and another in 1946. He then started making them in greater numbers and began selling them in 1947. Joe worked as an underground coal miner in Southern Illinois and found call making an excellent creative outlet and now finds it a way to fill the hours since retirement. Joe has been making calls since his first year of production in 1947 for sale and trade. As many call makers, he trades a lot of calls and has a fine collection from many modern makers and many of these calls were shown in the front part of the book.

How many calls he has made is a good question. He said probably around 2,000, but that is a guess. It seems like there were that many made by him on display in his display room! Price range for his calls is generally from $50 – $400. I purchased a nice cross-section of Jaroski calls because I really liked the quality of them. The photos show them in some detail in both the front of the book and again here. I really like the corncob calls the best as I am an old farmer and they remind me of decoy corn. Joe was inspired by a corncob call made by Tom Swanson of Iowa and he has added his own distinctive traits to that pattern.

Joe also created some beer bottle calls that were featured earlier in the book. Since he retired from mining at age 62 his creations keep him busy most every day due to his love for call making and for coming up with different and new ideas. All of Joe's beer bottle calls are working calls, both duck and goose. A few years ago Joe also made a dozen miniature working beer bottle calls with decals with his name on each of them. He made these in 1987 or 1988 and sold six of them. The other six Janice made a little carton for and labeled it "Joe's 6 Pak." It is not for sale but is seen in the photos shown previously.

Joe has won a number of awards, including blue, purple, orange, and red ribbons for call making from the Callmakers & Collectors Association of America. These include many ribbons (seen in photos) for Fancy Call Contest, Checkered Division Fancy Call, Miniature Fancy Call, Matched Sets, and more. He also took the Best Exhibit award plaque in 1994 and the 1995 Most Outstanding Exhibitor's Booth award at the Reelfoot Lake Callmakers & Collectors Association.

Joe Jaroski, Jr., signed duck call from 1954 and details showing the early metal reed on the 1954 call. Author's collection. $150

Joe Jaroski miniature working duck call. $25+

Fancy checkered call from Joe Jaroski with gold label. $125+

Two fancy Jaroski calls, both duck, inlaid checker-board design and inlaid ringed version. Checkerboard shows the gold label once used by Joe. $150+ each

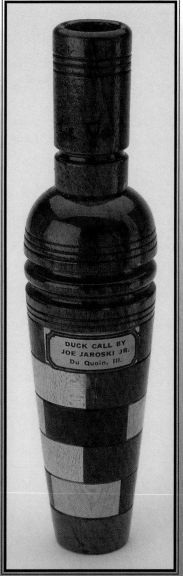

Walnut Joe Jaroski call made with napkin ring, name engraved on ring. $75+

A 1957 fox call made by Joe Jaroski with carved rings. $75+

One of Joe's newest designs, a square goose and duck call with engraved rings. $50+ each

KUMDUCK

This green plastic duck call with a plastic reed is manufactured similar to an Olt in style but out of plastic material. It is marked with a patent number of 2,711,614 and location. I have owned only three of them to date. According to the patent data, the call was made circa 1955. The patent was applied for on May 5, 1952, and granted on June 28, 1955, to Gordon E. Hallsten of Beaverton, Oregon. According to the patent application, the main purpose was to construct a call that took little effort to blow and used a straight reed construction. The call is all plastic, again, the material of the hour in 1952 when the patent was requested.

All I have to add about this little known company is that all three calls I have owned have come from contacts in the Pacific Northwest and I have never seen one here in the great duck hunting area of the Great Lakes Region. It is clearly similar to an Olt type and clearly marked as to what it is on the main call barrel. I believe the call may have been originally issued with a small diameter cord lanyard as shown below.

KumDuck duck call, Beaverton, Oregon, circa 1955. Author's collection. $50+

LOHMAN

Lohman calls were first located in Kansas City, Missouri, and later moved to Neosho, Missouri. Lohman marketed its calls through wholesalers to sporting goods dealers and the calls were also sold through many major catalog publications such as Stoeger's. Lohman advertised quite heavily in the sporting magazines also. Many of the calls themselves are not marked but usually the reed holder inserts were marked. Boxes and inserts will often give hints as to the different dates of the calls, with the Kansas City 27 address being an earlier company address. In 1957 the company was located at 3801-03 East 18th Street, Kansas City, Missouri, and one will find calls and stems marked "Kansas City 27, MO"; "Kansas City MO"; and, "Neosho, MO."

I have included information on the calls and model numbers below to serve as benchmarks for collectors to identify and log calls in production during different years. By examining wholesale catalogs and box inserts along with magazine advertising, one can reconstruct the calls being offered at any given time and I hope this helps the collector locate all of the various models of Lohman calls.

The *Shooter's Bible* by Stoeger Arms Corporation for 1966 shows the following Lohman calls available:
1. Lohman Duck Call No. 103
2. Lohman Crow Call No. 104
3. Lohman Squirrel Call No. 109
4. Lohman Chukar Call No. 117
5. Lohman Turkey Call No. 110
6. Lohman Predator Call No. 111
7. Lohman Goose Call No. 112
8. Lohman Deluxe Crow Call No. 106
9. Lohman Quail Call No. 115
10. Lohman Duck Call No. 200
11. Lohman Goose Call No. 201
12. Lohman Coon Talker No. 118

The 103, 104, 112, 106, 200, and 201 are not marked on the barrels. All other calls are clearly marked on the barrels. The Chukar and Squirrel are nearly identical and both sound a lot like squirrel chatter when one pushes the rubber air bellows on the end of the call. The difference between the two crow calls is the quality of the wood, with the 106 being hardwood. In 1966 these were plastic reed calls but they work very well and adjust easily. These calls are found often with the chukar, quail, and turkey being hardest to find.

Point Sporting Goods Company, a major wholesaler from Stevens Point, Wisconsin, in its 1981 catalog still carried the Lohman Crow Call but claimed the No. 104 was now black walnut with a cherry insert, which would indicate the No. 106 had become the No. 104. The wholesale cost was $4.90 in 1981. Other Lohman calls carried by Point in 1981 included: No. 103 Duck Call at $4.90; a cherrywood No. 420 Lohman-Bill Harper Deluxe Duck Call with double reeds at $11.60 wholesale; No. 430 Lohman-Bill Harper Marsh Call in walnut/cherrywood at $11.60; No. 440 Lohman-Bill Harper Wood Duck Call in walnut/cherrywood at $4.90; No. 109 Squirrel Call at $4.90; No. 112 Goose Call at $4.90; advertised as new, a No. 31 Deer Call at $4.90; advertised as new, two new turkey calls, Diaphragm type No. 802 at $3.35 and a box call with hinged lid, No. 870 at $13.40. Point also stocked two Lohman call cassettes, No. 51 Duck Calling and No. 50 Goose Calling, for $6.75 and $7.15 respectively.

An examination of the above shows a number of calls no longer offered and a number of new ones being offered beginning in the early eighties. Thus, without packaging, it is difficult to precisely date the calls but this at least gives a range of availability from 1966 until 1981. Lohman Calls predate 1966 and were widely sold and distributed in the 1950s. One interesting note about Point catalog advertising is that by the 1980s many calls were being associated with an individual's name, such as the Bill Harper

Deluxe Duck Call. In other words, Lohman was trying to capitalize on the rebirth of the role and importance of the individual carvers in our new golden age of call making.

Values on Lohman calls will depend on rarity and condition, boxed or loose. I would rate the boxed calls at $25 minimum up to $100 for some of the rarer calls in boxes. The loose calls would bring about 50% of that value for the most part.

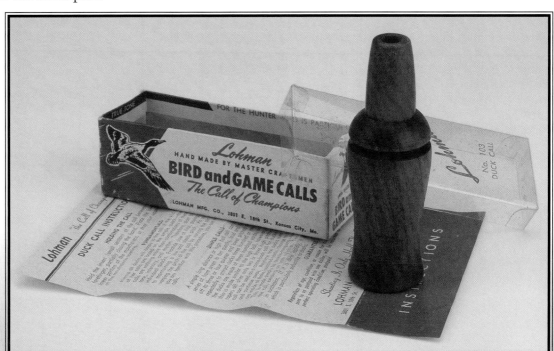

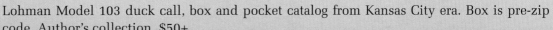

Lohman Model 103 duck call, box and pocket catalog from Kansas City era. Box is pre-zip code. Author's collection. $50+

Lohman Model 112 goose call, Neosho, Missouri, call, box, and instructions. Author's collection. $35 due to rough shape of box and call.

Two Lohman crow calls. Author's collection. $25 – 40 each

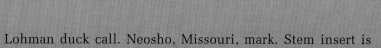

Lohman duck call. Neosho, Missouri, mark. Stem insert is also marked "Lohman, Neosho, MO." Author's collection. $40

Lohman duck call (large), marked "Neosho" on stem only. Author's collection. $40

Lohman goose call, Neosho, Missouri. Model only marked on stem. This is actually smaller than the duck call shown in the photo on the right. Author's collection. $40

LYNCH'S

Lynch's has distributed many turkey calls and is one of the more common mass-producer of calls for turkey hunting. The calls are well made and have a nice sound. The one shown has called in a few of the old bearded birds for me.

Author's personal Model 150 Lynch's Long Beard turkey call, box style. $35 – 50

MALLARDTONE GAME CALLS

Mallardtone Game Calls began commercial production in 1955 when "Ole" Oluf H. Rasmussen (1894 – 1973) and William Rasmussen (1927) began making calls together for sale and the company was officially launched in 1957. Ole had experimented with metal reed calls in the 1940s and both Ole and Bill had won calling championships in the 1950s and 1960s, including crow, goose, and duck calling competitions. The operation began in Ole's basement in Rock Island, Illinois, and moved to 4th Street in Moline, Illinois, in 1960. In 1965 they were located at 16th Street also in Moline. The earliest calls indeed had metal but within four years all calls changed to vinyl reeds.

The stamping for Mallardtone only changed once since the beginning of production but the plastic wedgeblocks (Mallardtone always used plastic wedgeblocks) were red in color until 1965 and then changed to yellow. Clearly they also used green at some point as shown in the photo in the front of the book. Most of the calls were made of walnut but during the 1960s some calls were also made of cocobola and sumac. They also made no more than six calls of ebony. The original duck call was Model M-5 and the M-295 was the less expensive call made in 1965. Today the grandson is still running the business at 10406 96th Street Court West, Taylor Ridge, IL 61284.

Much of this information comes from a Mallardtone collector kind enough to share his knowledge. There is also an interesting connection between Charles Bishop (featured earlier) and Mallardtone with Strombeck & Becker of East Moline, Illinois, turning barrels and inserts for both companies.

I did not start finding advertising for the calls in wholesale catalogs until the late 1950s and early 1960s. One magazine advertisement from 1962 indicates that the company won the National Crow Calling Contest in 1962, both first and second place (Bill Rasmussen). The same advertising indicated that they had won "…numerous other championships with duck and goose calls" (Ole had finished second once and fifth three times in the 1950s – 1960s). The address given for the company in 1962 was 2100 Stadium Drive, Dept. 962, Rock Island, Illinois. Canadian Sauer Ltd., 103 Church Street, Toronto, Canada, also distributed the calls in Canada.

In 1962 the company offered crow, predator, squirrel, duck, goose, deer, and pheasant calls. In addition, Deluxe model duck and goose calls were available for $10.00, twice the price of the other duck and goose calls. The other calls were all $2.95 each (Model M-295). An instruction record was also available for $2.00. All calls came with unconditional guarantees.

However, like other modern calls, one does not often find these calls in pristine condition in their packages. As a matter of fact, I have most of the Mallardtone calls and do not have packages. Possibly they were marketed in bulk through wholesalers in addition to being individually packaged. I know this was the case with some of the less expensive fishing lure lines. However, I have confirmed they were also individually packaged.

I like the calls myself and find them well made with excellent finishes. Also, the engraving gives them a nice distinction from other mass marketed calls. The advertising in Buckeye Sports Supply catalog said: "Made of finest materials available. The barrel (or body) of each call is American Black Walnut, assuring beauty and lasting durability. All calls are hand tested by an expert." The wholesaler offered the following calls in 1982:

1. Mallardtone M-5 DC Duck Call
2. Mallardtone M-296 DCJ Duck Call
3. Mallardtone M-5 GC Goose Call
4. Mallardtone M-295 CC Goose Call
5. Mallardtone Close Range Predator Call M-295 CRPC
6. Mallardtone Predator Call M-295 PC
7. Mallardtone Squirrel Call M-295 SC (wood/bellows)
8. Mallardtone Turkey Call M-395 TC (box type)
9. Mallardtone Hawk Call M-295 HC
10. Mallardtone Deer Call M-295 DrC
11. Mallardtone Pheasant Call M-295 PhC
12. Mallardtone Coon Call M-350 CoC

The squirrel call was wood with rubber bellows on the end. Not all calls had stoppers: predator calls, deer, or pheasant; a deer call is shown on page 150 for example. Again, these calls are well made and attractive due to the engraving on them. Each call is clearly marked as to type of call and many have engravings of the animal being pursued, e.g. a duck, coon, fox, or squirrel. Collectors must make their own collecting decisions but for my money I like these calls a lot. Apparently so do other collectors as they have fairly high collector values already. I would look for the red wedgeblocks to indicate the pre-1965 models and a real treat would be finding an early metal reed version from the 1950s.

Mint Mallardtone deer call.
Author's collection. $50

Two Mallardtone duck calls and the details of one showing the yellow plastic
wedge, reed, and stem details. Author's collection. $50+ each

Mallardtone goose call.
Author's collection. $50+

Mallardtone fox call. Note it is made without a stopper
similar to the deer call. Author's collection. $50+

KEN MARTIN

Although not as prodigious as some of the larger companies, Ken Martin marketed a beautiful duck and goose call through a number of outlets, including major wholesalers. He also advertised his calls nationally. The 1970 Cabela's catalog offered his Model KMG (Ken Martin Goose) call for $10 and his Model KMD (Ken Martin Duck) call for $5. Both of these calls were clearly marked on the barrels so the collector will have no trouble identifying them. This is an example of a vintage call maker responding to mass-marketing pressures to sell his calls. The Martin calls are very collectible and would command at least $100 each, likely more. Mr. Martin is deceased and his calls will continue to appreciate. He first produced calls in Illinois (as seen in Jaroski collection) and then moved to Idaho.

Ken Martin goose call made while he lived in Idaho Falls, Idaho. Author's collection. $200

NATURAL DUCK CALL MANUFACTURING COMPANY

I cannot think of a collector of duck calls not wanting a call that looks like a duck! This is a very unique and desirable call from the 1930s that was manufactured in St. Paul, Minnesota. The call has a nice sound and details are shown below with the call in the closed and open bill positions. According to Donna Tonelli, Francis J. Muchlistein patented it in 1932 and there are early calls that are simply marked "Patent Applied" so be aware of this variation. She shows the call and paperwork in her *Top of the Line Hunting Collectibles* book on page 194. I think she undervalues the call in her book and that it is worth twice the $300 she suggests, or more.

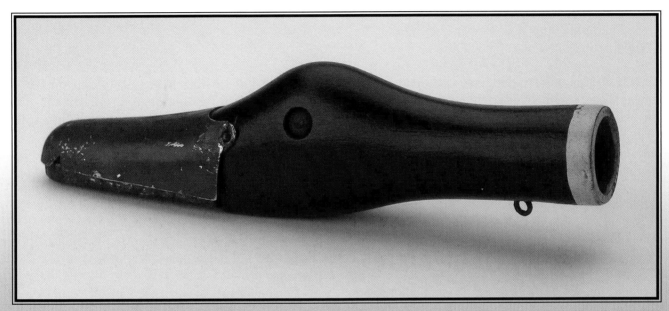

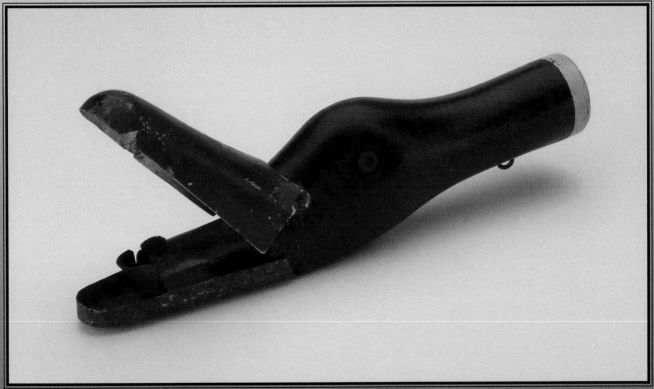

Natural duck call in both the open and closed positions. Author's collection. $600+

PERFECTONE

Charlie Bishop was already discussed and some of his calls were shown in the Jaroski collection. He originally made calls in Arkansas in the 1930s and 1940s and then moved to Davenport, Iowa, in 1950 where he continued his call production. He lived from 1912 – 2001. He had made calls many of his 89 years of life and produced highly collectible calls of fine quality.

Also, as mentioned previously, it appears that Strombeck & Becker of East Moline, Illinois, turned some of the barrels and inserts for both Charlie and Mallardtone. Mr. Bishop was a very prolific call maker and his calls are well known in the upper Midwest and highly desired by collectors. His calls were shown in detail earlier.

P. S. OLT

P. S. Olt was briefly discussed as an example of an individual Illinois River Style call maker. Olt calls are likely the most recognizable calls of all to even the beginning collector due to being manufactured primarily of hard rubber and all being clearly marked as to maker. Olt began a revolution in call making by using hard rubber to manufacture calls, and this company, located in Pekin, Illinois, is still in business today. The biggest challenge to an Olt collector is dating with accuracy any of the hard rubber calls. There are some clues in addresses, model numbers on calls, logos on calls, shape of stoppers, etc.; however, even many fairly recent Olt calls command over $50 if still found in the original packaging. An individual could, and many do, concentrate on just Olt calls and never get bored looking for a new one.

Olt, like Herter's, made every conceivable call. Some of the calls are harder to find than others. They also made "Junior Models," not for kids, just smaller sized calls, that are rarer and command premium prices, often selling for $100 plus. Olt calls are plentiful because they were excellent calls when first made and still are. In addition to hunting ducks, I have been an avid squirrel hunter ever since my now departed dog Bandit treed his first squirrel back in 1983 until his death in 1996. Bandit "loved to hate" those pesky little devils that used to bug him in our backyard. One day I, in addition to Bandit, discovered the Olt Perfect Squirrel Call shown on page 160 in black and brown. The black one I picked up at a farm auction but it turned out to be quite an old model sold from a now defunct Detroit, Michigan, sporting goods store. I used the black one for nearly 20 years with success each time I went to the woods. The calls are shown with the stopper purposely stuck in on the black one to show the operation of the automatic caller. Just push in on the end and the call sound is made automatically. Listed below are a number of Olt calls being sold at different periods to serve as a benchmark reference in Olt collecting.

According to Stoeger Arms Corporation's *The Shooter's Bible* for 1947, Olt had been making the famous D-2 Duck Call for 40 years (1907). Businesses were just gearing up again after the war years and the offerings were meager in 1947 by most companies. Olt offered only seven calls, available through Stoeger Arms:

1. Model D-2 Duck Call, wholesale price of $1.50
2. Model E-1 Crow Call, wholesale price of $1.50
3. Model A-5 Goose Call at $3.50
4. Model B-4 Adjustable Bird Call at $2.75
5. Model C-3 Mallard Call at $2.50
6. Model G-7 Hawk Call at $1.50
7. Model F-6 Turkey cedar box call at $1.50

The Shooter's Bible for 1966 listed the following Olt calls:
1. Model E-1 Crow
2. Model M-9 Crow
3. Model B-10 Squirrel
4. Model S-8 Perfect Squirrel
5. Model W-12 Pintail/Widgeon
6. Model D-2 Duck
7. Model G-7 Hawk
8. Model L-22 Goose
9. Model A-5 Perfect Goose
10. Model A-50 Canada Honker
11. Model R-25 Perfect Deer
12. Model T-20 Fox/Coyote
13. Model N-27 Perfect Coon
14. Model F-6 Turkey box call
15. Model Q-30 Quail
16. Model 500 Chukar
17. Model O-32 Pheasant

The 1970 Cabela's catalog offered the following:
1. Mark V wooden Duck Call
2. Model 33 wooden Predator Call
3. Model A-50 Honker Call
4. Model Q-30 Quail Call
5. Model EL-45 Elk Call
6. Model S-8 Perfect Squirrel
7. Model N-27 Coon Call
8. Model R-25 Deer Call
9. Model CP-21 Close Range Predator
10. Model F-6 Two Tone Turkey Call

The 1981 Point wholesale catalog had the following available:
1. Model E-1 Crow Call
2. Model 400 Wood Crow Call
3. Model 32 Pheasant Call
4. Model D-2 Duck Call
5. Model 66 Wooden Duck Call
6. Model 200 Wooden Duck Call
7. Model B-10 Squirrel Call
8. Model S-8 Perfect Squirrel Call
9. Model 300 Wood Goose Call
10. Model A-5 Goose Call
11. Model A-50 Canadian Honker
12. Model 77 Wood Goose Call
13. Model T-20 Fox/Coyote Call
14. Model R-25 Perfect Deer Call
15. #90 Game Call Holder
16. D100 Mallard Records
17. G101 Goose Records

The 1982 Buckeye Sports Supply wholesale catalog listed the following Olt calls for sale:
1. Model D-2 Duck
2. Model E-1 Crow
3. Model T-20 Predator
4. Model B-10 Squirrel
5. Model L-22 Goose
6. Model 44 Crow (wood)
7. Model 33 Predator (wood)
8. Model 99M Duck (wood/metal reed)
9. Model Mark V Duck (wood)
10. Model DR-115 Duck (wood)
11. Model F-6 Turkey (box type)
12. Model GB-110 Turkey (box/lid)
13. Model N-27 Coon
14. Model EL-45 Elk
15. Model 600 Deer (wood)
16. Model 800 Goose (wood)
17. Also three lanyard types

By 1970, Olt began to distribute more and more wooden calls to capitalize on the revived interest in American game calls produced in natural wood, e.g. the new golden age of call making and emphasis on individual call makers. The 1970 Cabela's catalog offered only ten Olt calls, but three of them were in wood: the Mark V Duck Call, the Model 33 Predator Call, and the Two Tone Turkey Call. An examination of the Parker Distributors Catalog from 1970 shows a complete line of 27 Olt calls and even more wooden duck and goose calls. These, along with other wooden Olt calls such as the Model 66 and Model 77 are already quite collectible. A comparison of just these catalog years shows the extensive possibilities of putting together a nice P. S. Olt collection. Even the differences between 1981 and 1982 are immense, with many new wooden calls being available in 1982. Most Olt calls are affordable but there are some rarer ones out there commanding over $100. However, most of the calls will bring between $25 – $75 loose, maybe double with clean, crisp boxes and any inserts that came with the calls.

The values given above are obviously a very general range, and one must remember there are some short production run calls that will command premium prices. There are also color variations, logo variations, presence of lanyard ring variations, and many other items to learn about with Olt calls, all of which affect valuation. Given my personal and extensive experience with modern fishing lures, I am certain that there are some Olt calls that will start commanding some very premium prices once we have documented their rarity and once the demand increases even more by additional collectors entering the hobby. A person could concentrate on just Olt calls and keep very busy indeed building an exemplary collection from early call making through the modern era.

Olt Canadian Honker Call, Tri-County special issue numbered 142. Author's collection. $75

Olt D-2 Duck Call, Tri-County special issue numbered 142 to match goose call. Author's collection. $75

Map diagram on the 1995 special issue calls by Olt.

Olt Chukar Call, wood/rubber, worn lettering. Author's collection. $40

Olt T-20 black barrel, green stem Predator Call in a post-zip code green and yellow box with a cellophane insert common in 1960s – early 1970s. This is the box that was just before the yellow hang box shown below with the M-9 crow call. Author's collection. $50+

Olt M-9 Crow Call new in package. This packaging was being advertised as early as 1970, Author's collection. $50 in package

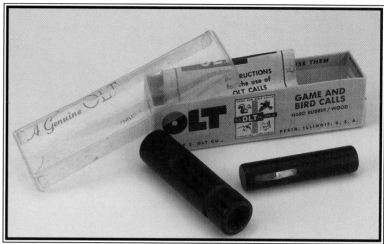

Olt W-12 pintail whistle/call in cardboard box with plastic top, pre-zip code, details of box graphics shown along with internal parts of call. This box pre-dates the two types on page 158. Author's collection. $75 boxed

Olt 0-32 Regular Pheasant Call, black barrel with red stem. Author's collection. $50+

Olt B-10 Squirrel Call in same hang package as the M-9 on page 158. Author's collection. $50 in package

My personal Perfect Squirrel Call by Olt with a black barrel showing the end stopper pushed in and an early Detroit, Michigan, sporting goods store label. These are also found in brown as shown below. Author's collection. $125+

Brown Perfect Squirrel Call by Olt. Author's collection. $100+

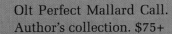

Olt Perfect Mallard Call. Author's collection. $75+

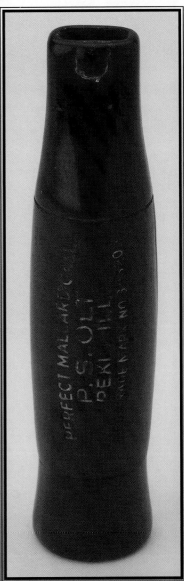

Two Olt Junior Hawk calls.
Author's collection. $75+ each

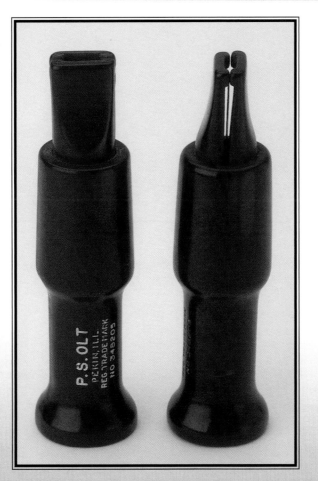

Olt Model Perfect Mallard Duck
Call with lanyard ring, keyhole
pattern. Author's collection. $100

Details of the Olt W-12 Pintail Whistle/Call from page 159. $75

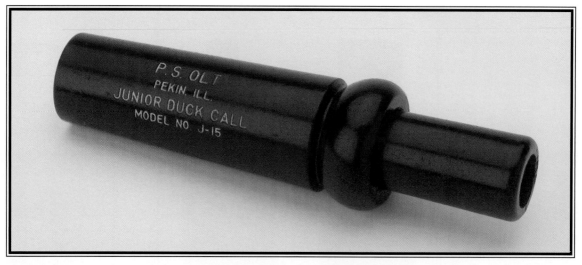

Olt Model J-15, Junior Duck Call. Author's collection. $100+

Olt Perfect Goose Call. Author's collection. $50 – 75

Olt Model D-2 Duck Call with trademark on stem. $40

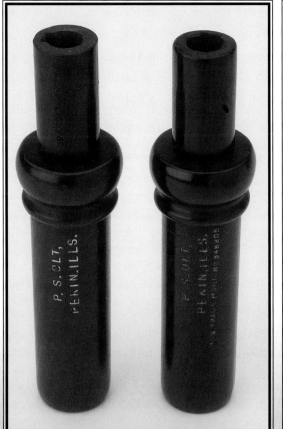

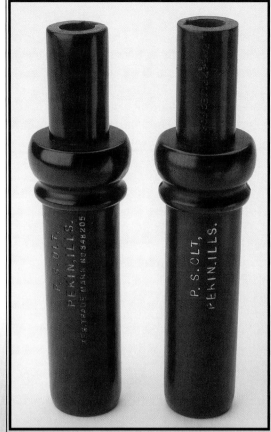

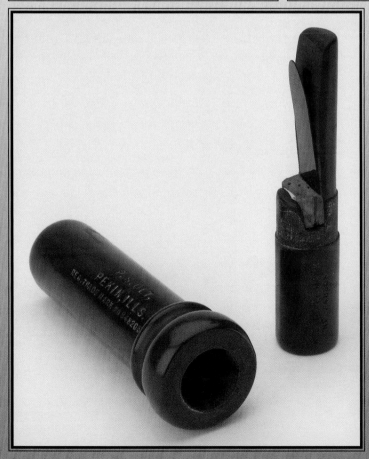

Olt Model D-2 Duck Calls and the details of an Olt stem showing the cork wedge and the reed. One of the calls is the earlier keyhole design on the stem end and is a bit more valuable. However, D-2s were made in very large numbers. Author's collection. $40 – 60 each

SCOTCH

With maternal grandparents named McQueen and McIlvain I cannot help but include these calls! Scotch game calls were designed with bellows attached to wooden calls that would make the appropriate sound when air movement through the reed was generated by the bellows and not the caller. They are calls constructed in the fashion of a regular wooden call, shaped similar to many Lohman calls, with rubber bellows placed over the mouthpiece of the call for air inlet. When the bellows move and emit air the call sound is produced. They call anytime one moves the bellows, including while walking or moving around if not careful. This could indeed be an unwanted noise emitted at just the wrong time in the blind.

However, it is a neat idea that was apparently new in commercial production about 1955. An advertisement for the duck call (Patent Pending) appeared in the October 1955 *Outdoor Life*. The call was available for $7.50 and only duck, goose, and crow calls were available in 1955. The company address was 173 Victor Avenue, Dept. L10, Detroit 3, Mich. The L10 likely stood for the advertising source (e.g. *Outdoor Life*, October with the code L for *Outdoor Life* and 10 for October) to track sales similar to how Pratt Decoys used different names in advertising.

I have shown Scotch Predator Call No. 1503 new in its box, Duck Call No. 1401, and Goose Call No. 1605. They also made a Crow Call No. 1707 and a Squirrel Call No. 1911. A wholesale catalog also listed a Deer Call No. 1809 advertised in 1968 that must have been short-lived indeed. The interesting thing that I noted on the Predator call shown is that the call itself is imprinted with a Detroit, Michigan, address and so was the box originally. However, on the box, Detroit was crossed out and the New York address added without a zip code. The booklet inside the box had the New York address with zip code. The duck and goose calls shown have the New York imprint on them. The calls were invented in Detroit and produced there briefly. Thus, the Detroit calls are harder to find. I have owned all but the Squirrel Call and do not see it listed in as many wholesale catalogs.

If one removes the bellows, the calls function just fine if one knows how to blow them. The value on these is between $25 and $60, depending on age, box type, and condition. The 1970 Cabela's catalog offered all five models at $4.75 each. The 1982 Buckeye Sports Supply wholesale catalog still offered the duck, goose, predator, and crow calls for $7.55 – $8.95 each wholesale. They also offered a double or single Scotch Lanyard at that time. Retail on these calls was an average of about $12.50 in 1982, so expect to pay double for even one of the early 1980s models. As noted already, the Squirrel Call did not appear in the 1982 wholesale catalog so it is likely more difficult to find, along with the deer call.

Scotch predator call, Model 1503, made in Detroit, Michigan, but Detroit is marked out on address on box and corrected to 60 Main Street, Oakfield, NY, in lower left corner of box. The paper insert also includes the zip code of 14125 but it is not on the box, demonstrating the call must be from the era when zip codes were first being used. The Detroit calls would be earliest and most difficult to locate. Author's collection. $50.00+

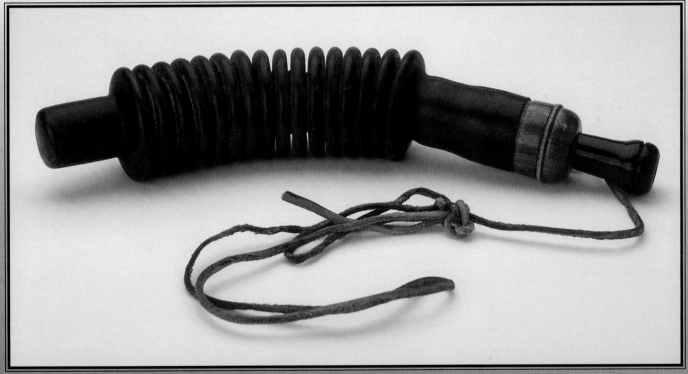

A. Scotch duck call. The rubber is marked Oakfield, N. Y. The duck call is Model No. 1401. Author's collection. $40

B. Scotch goose call, Oakfield, N. Y., Model 1605. Author's collection. $40

SMITH'S GAME CALLS

Smith's Game Calls of Summerville, Pennsylvania, is a productive regional company. The call shown was a gift from Ron Kommer, a friend of mine familiar with calls that also did a bit of writing for sporting magazines. The striker fits snugly into the sound chamber. Some sandpaper is glued to the striker to keep slate lightly buffed. In use one simply unwinds the cord and flips over the back of the neck, allowing the box to dangle on one side with the striker on the other. To call, cradle the box lightly in one hand with the hole facing outward and the back of the hand resting against one's tummy (but not the box). The striker is held like a pencil just off of vertical. Just about any sound a hen turkey makes can be achieved with only a little practice. One drawback with the call is that one cannot get the slate wet or it will not work properly. Smith's also made a glass striker that will work when the slate's wet.

Two views of the Model
T-12 Turkey Caller. $50+

THOMPSON

Similar to Ken Martin discussed earlier, Tom Thompson made vintage calls and then marketed his calls nationally at a later time. He made calls using both wood and plastics and his plastic goose call is an excellent call with a superb sound. Most of his earlier calls from Illinois bring from $50 – $150 at this time. Thompson was first located in Illinois and then later moved to Idaho.

Thompson T-550 goose call, Boise, Idaho, green plastic reed. Author's collection. $50

Beautiful TRUTONE call, circa 1930s. Author's collection. $400+

TRUTONE

Some of the most beautiful modern calls were made by the call making company headed by call maker L. G. Larson (1888 – 1947). Many of these calls were made with curly maple, special burl walnut, or a combination, as shown here. The calls were normally marked on the top of the sound barrels in lettering in an arc marked "TRUTONE" on the top linewith "Oak Park, Ill." underneath it. A collector finding a TRUTONE call is lucky indeed and has a valuable factory call to add to his collection.

UNKNOWN CALLS

There are a few calls shown of which I do not know the manufacturer. They are all without markings and/or I could not verify them in advertising literature or other texts. Again, if a reader recognizes the call, please let me know so I can pass the data along to other collectors in the future.

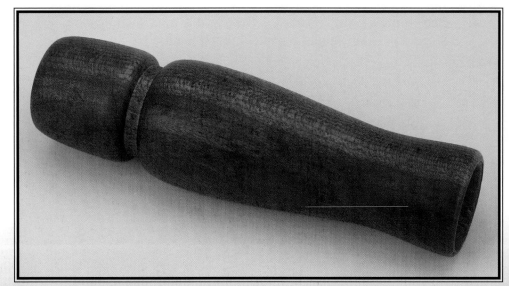

Predator call with plastic disk insert with four holes, works well. Author's collection. $25+

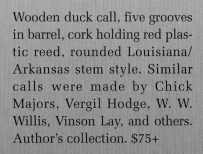

Wooden duck call, five grooves in barrel, cork holding red plastic reed, rounded Louisiana/Arkansas stem style. Similar calls were made by Chick Majors, Vergil Hodge, W. W. Willis, Vinson Lay, and others. Author's collection. $75+

Large plastic reed, very long stem, wooden goose call, three grooves in barrel. Author's collection. $75+

Details of an unknown duck call. Author's collection. $40+

Wild Life Predator Call. Author's collection. $25+

Literature on Calls

As Luckey pointed out in 1992, there was an increasing interest in calls as collectibles but very little formal written material on call collecting at that time. However, some of the early works were just beginning to appear then: (1) *Duck Calls and Other Game Calls* by Brian McGrath (1988); (2) *Reelfoot Lake, History-Duck Call Makers-Hunting Tales* by Russell Caldwell (1989); and (3) *Duck Calls, An Enduring American Folk Art* by Howard Harlan and W. Crew Anderson (1988).

Unlike books on collecting decoys (there are well over 100), the above three titles, Luckey's earlier work, and a few magazine articles in *Ducks Unlimited* magazine and *American Shotgunner* were all the publications available on calls until recently. In 1994, a book on general game calls was released and Harlan also published a turkey call book. You should have a copy of each in your library, but as Harlan and Anderson say about information regarding duck calls: "Some of this story has been lost. Until now, no one thought it important enough to research and write down."

The development of the art and science of call making has reached new high points. The calling contests and contestants have constantly demanded finer and finer instruments and this has resulted in the high quality, technologically advanced calls produced by makers today. Unbelievably, they are still improving them. The final quality of a call is found, however, in the ability of the hunter to use it. A fine call does not a fine caller make, and used wrongly it not only lessens your chances at bagging a limit, but it also may prevent the hunter from bagging any birds at all. Bad calls and callers can, at the very least, make friends unhappy and nearby hunters downright angry. The latter have been known to express their dissatisfaction in most unpleasant words and actions and, if you persist in driving the birds away, the former may become the latter, making it very difficult to find hunting companions.

Although quality and versatility of the sounds capable of being made on a call can certainly have a bearing on its collectibility, it is more important with contemporary calls than with older ones. This is the reason that it is given short shrift in this presentation. Most of the old calls that survived probably were as effective as were needed or required at the time, or they probably would not have survived. However, sound quality is something many collectors also admire in a call and they would prefer a quality sound over an inferior one.

Since the early 1990s there has been somewhat of an explosion of information available on calls and call making. This is in part due to the two associations of call makers and collectors. But it is also due to the increased interest in call collecting and the advent of the Internet. A simple search on one's favorite Internet search engine will result in numerous hits on calls and call making, and one will find plenty of information available on the Internet to begin a decent education on the art of game calls. Many individual makers also have websites touting their own wares and giving their own history of call making. The books listed below are a beginning point for the serious collector. Unfortunately, many are now out of print and are themselves collector items, costing a bit more than normal for a book of this nature:

Collecting Antique Bird Decoys and Duck Calls, 3rd Edition, by Carl F. Luckey and Russell E. Lewis. Copyright 2003 by Krause Publications and Russell E. Lewis. Paperback, 8½" x 11", 496 pages. Signed and numbered copies available from the author or any major bookstore. This is my book so I will not say it is great, but it is. Luckey was of course one of the first to discuss the role and importance of duck calls in America and I was fortunate enough to be selected to fully update and rewrite his earlier book, and I added major sections on modern calls and many new items on calls and call making. I may be contacted at findingo@netonecom.net or through my website at http://www.wwbait.net at any time.

Duck Calls and Other Game Calls by Brian J. McGrath. Copyright 1988. The Thomas B. Reel Company, 2005 Tree House, Piano, TX 75023. Hardbound, 8" x 10½", 150 pages. A very good guide to collecting calls. Well illustrated with descriptive entries of makers and the characteristics and styles of their products. This book was issued in a limited edition of 950 and Luckey's copy, purchased in early 1991, was numbered 947. This edition is out of print.

Duck Calls-An Enduring American Folk Art by Howard L. Harlan and W. Crew Anderson. Copyright 1988. Harlan Anderson Press, 4920 Franklin Road, Nashville, TN 37220. Hardbound, 8½" x 11", 316 pages. An exhaustive and scholarly study of the American duck call and its history. This large limited edition book is a must for anyone interested in collecting duck calls. Harlan and Anderson obviously devoted considerable time to the research, photography, and writing of this very fine book. One of the best books available on duck calls and duck calling.

Reelfoot Lake, History-Duck Call Makers-Hunting Tales, Revised Edition, by Russell H. Caldwell. Copyright 1989. Caldwell's Office Outfitters, Inc., Union City, TN 38261. Hardbound, 5½" x 8½", 272 pages. Anyone interested in Reelfoot Lake Style duck calls could not possibly do without this book. Written by a native and lifetime resident of the area, hunter and sportsman Caldwell has compiled what has to be the definitive work on the history and identification of duck calls and their makers of the Reelfoot Lake area. Now out of print.

Ducks, How To Call Them by Tom Turpin. Copyright date unknown. This is an old 50-page softbound, 5½" x 8½" booklet that is interesting and chock-full of calling advice. What makes it useful is Turpin's drawing and specifications for his calls. A softcover reprint from 1987 is available.

Duck Calling by Earl Dennison. Copyright date unknown. This is another old 5" x 7½", softbound 60-page booklet. Anyone interested in the history of duck calls should try to obtain a copy. Luckey got his from W. F. "Tom" Dennison, Earl's son, who runs Dennison Sporting Goods, Box 116, Hwy 51 South, Newbern, TN.

Fish and Fowl Decoys of the Great Lakes by Donna Tonelli. Copyright 2002 by Donna Tonelli and published by Schiffer Publishing Ltd., 4880 Lower Valley Road, Atglen, PA 19310. A wonderful book on decoys with quite a few calls of the Midwestern region shown, which of course includes many fine makers. Available from the author or publisher.

Top of the Line Hunting Collectibles by Donna Tonelli. Copyright 1999 by Donna Tonelli and published also by Schiffer. This is a must-have for every decoy and calls collector and features high-end calls and decoys, including fine sections on advertising items and related hunting collectibles. This book is full color with excellent illustrations, and it adds extensive historical detail on many items not covered in other books to date.

One Internet site for call books is http://huntingrigbooks.com and is owned by Dean and Shirley Dashner. The Dashners had the following books for sale on their site as of December 19, 2002:

Bowman: *Arkansas Duck Hunters Almanac*, 1988 softcover, hardcover

Christensen, Robert D.: *Duck Calls of Illinois, 1863 – 1963*. 1993

Cost: *The Gobbler's Shop-How to Make Turkey Calls*, 1999, out of print

Cost & Meo: *Cost Talks Turkey*, 2000

Fleming, James C., Jr.: *Custom Calls, Duck & Goose Calls from Today's Craftsmen*, 1995

Harlan, Howard: *Turkey Calls-An Enduring American Folk Art*, 1994 (a book with which I am familiar and highly endorse for its history)

Mickle: *Call Makers Past and Present*, 1994, out of print

Mickle: *The Rest of the Best*, 1999

As can be seen from this list, even recent books on this art form tend to be out of print very quickly due to limited numbers being printed of each book. When you find a call book of interest, it's best to purchase it. In addition to the above, I would recommend an excellent chapter on calls in *Art Carver: The Sporting Craftsmen*, 1994, Countrysport Press, New Albany, Ohio. This book has chapters on many collectibles of interest, including calls, knives, and decoys. The call chapter is very well written with some fine modern call makers represented.

Also add to the above list a new book on predator calls: *Predator Calls The First 50 Years* by Al Lux and Jay Nistetter, available from the authors online via auction and at sporting collectibles shows. I have only quickly looked at this one but it appears extremely detailed and gives a lot of data on modern call companies as well.

Finally, there are indeed many fine books dealing with waterfowl hunting that have short sections on duck and goose calls and how to use them. Some of these books are very useful and even depict calls not seen any longer in some instances. In addition to the waterfowl books, general sporting collectibles books normally have at least a brief section on calls.

Other Books by Russell E. Lewis

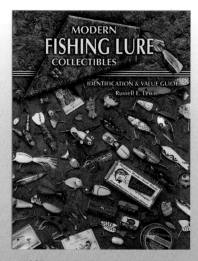

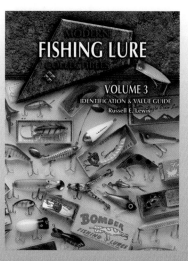

| 8½" x 11", 288 pgs., $24.95 | 8½" x 11", 304 pgs., $24.95 | 8½" x 11", 288 pgs., $24.95 |

Each of these volumes is a history, identification, and value guide for fishing lure collectibles from 1940 until the mid-1980s, including lures, reels, rods, decoys, and miscellaneous items. There are around 1,200 beautiful color photos and original catalog pages and advertisements in each volume. There are tips on collecting and dating techniques, as well as historical coverage of the changes that ultimately led to the closing or selling off of most major lure companies by 1988. Manufacturers include Heddon, Creek Chub, Shakespeare, and Paw Paw. Volume 2 covers more than 140 companies not in Volume 1, and a "field find" tackle box from the modern era. Volume 3 contains expanded information on companies that could not be fully covered in Volumes 1 and 2, as well as new companies: Horrocks-Ibbotson Company, Wood's Lures, L & S Minnows, and Cisco Kid Lures, to name just a few. While Volume 2 gave the complete history for nearly 50 years by examining vintage catalogs, Volume 3 shows many of the actual rods and reels in photos with approximate values for items from 1937 through 1952.

Volume 1 • Item #6028 • ISBN: 1-57432-277-X
8½ x 11 • 288 Pgs. • HB • 2002 values • $24.95
Volume 2 • Item #6131 • ISBN: 1-57432-304-0
8½ x 11 • 304 Pgs. • HB • 2003 values • $24.95
Volume 3 • Item #6564 • ISBN: 1-57432-422-5
8½ x 11 • 288 Pgs. • HB • 2005 values • $24.95

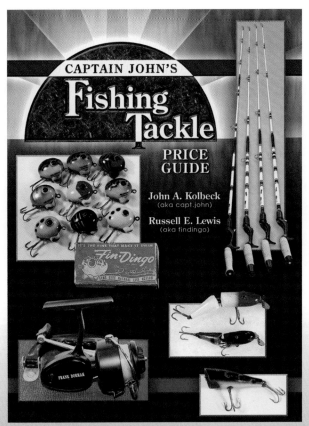

8½" x 11", 224 pgs., $19.95

Online dealers and collectors will delight in reeling in *Captain John's Fishing Tackle Price Guide*. Captain John, a.k.a. John Kolbeck, has been in the online fishing business for over 10 years and has sold thousands of items over the Internet — "Captain John" still spends up to 70 hours each week online buying and selling. His diligent record keeping has produced an amazing database of items and their actual selling prices which he and co-author Russell E. Lewis (a.k.a. "findingo" and author of Modern Fishing Lure Collectibles, Volumes 1 and 2) have compiled into this handy reference guide. Each listing in the book contains the name, model, description, maker, condition, selling price, and date of sale. There are over 10,000 listings, of which over 7,000 are lures. There are also rods, reels, tackle boxes, catalogs and vintage advertisements, and over 1,000 miscellaneous items. All this data in one easy-to-use guide allows readers to see sales trends and compare lure makes, models, and conditions. Captain John estimates that 10% of his annual sales are to overseas buyers, so the over 10,000 prices at your fingertips allow you to track sales changes over time on a global scale. Representative photographs of each category are also provided to aid collectors in identification. You'll be hooked when you snag *Capt. John's Fishing Tackle Price Guide*!

Field Guide to Fishing Lures is aimed at assisting the beginning, intermediate, and advanced collector and the general antique and collectible dealer in identifying both collectible older vintage lures and the more modern classic fishing lures. It contains a cross-section of both very old and more recent collectible lures and includes values for each lure shown. With the help of this easy-to-tote guide, collectors will be able to recognize all major categories of lures and the most significant companies in the industry while hunting for additions to their collections. The book begins with the six major companies, Creek Chub Bait Company, Heddon, Paw Paw, Pfleuger, Shakespeare, and South Bend. Then an alphabetical listing of more than 200 companies highlights other significant manufacturers and their major contributions. The book continues the tradition of high quality, detailed photographs useful in identifying small nuances important in lure collecting, as well as the author's practice of providing historical data for readers.

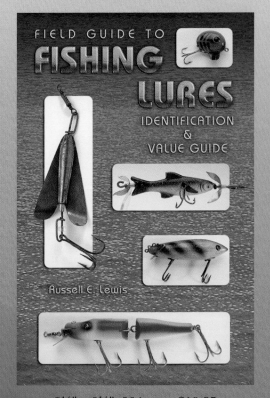

5½" x 8½", 224 pgs., $16.95

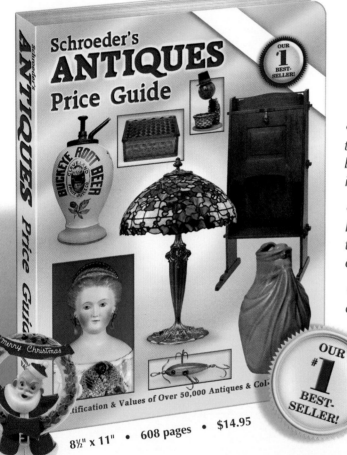